ADVANCES IN INFORMATION SECURITY MANAGEMENT & SMALL SYSTEMS SECURITY

IFIP - The International Federation for Information Processing

IFIP was founded in 1960 under the auspices of UNESCO, following the First World Computer Congress held in Paris the previous year. An umbrella organization for societies working in information processing, IFIP's aim is two-fold: to support information processing within its member countries and to encourage technology transfer to developing nations. As its mission statement clearly states,

IFIP's mission is to be the leading, truly international, apolitical organization which encourages and assists in the development, exploitation and application of information technology for the benefit of all people.

IFIP is a non-profitmaking organization, run almost solely by 2500 volunteers. It operates through a number of technical committees, which organize events and publications. IFIP's events range from an international congress to local seminars, but the most important are:

- The IFIP World Computer Congress, held every second year;
- open conferences;
- working conferences.

The flagship event is the IFIP World Computer Congress, at which both invited and contributed papers are presented. Contributed papers are rigorously refereed and the rejection rate is high.

As with the Congress, participation in the open conferences is open to all and papers may be invited or submitted. Again, submitted papers are stringently refereed.

The working conferences are structured differently. They are usually run by a working group and attendance is small and by invitation only. Their purpose is to create an atmosphere conducive to innovation and development. Refereeing is less rigorous and papers are subjected to extensive group discussion.

Publications arising from IFIP events vary. The papers presented at the IFIP World Computer Congress and at open conferences are published as conference proceedings, while the results of the working conferences are often published as collections of selected and edited papers.

Any national society whose primary activity is in information may apply to become a full member of IFIP, although full membership is restricted to one society per country. Full members are entitled to vote at the annual General Assembly, National societies preferring a less committed involvement may apply for associate or corresponding membership. Associate members enjoy the same benefits as full members, but without voting rights. Corresponding members are not represented in IFIP bodies. Affiliated membership is open to non-national societies, and individual and honorary membership schemes are also offered.

ADVANCES IN INFORMATION SECURITY MANAGEMENT & SMALL SYSTEMS SECURITY

IFIP TC11 WG11.1/WG11.2
Eighth Annual Working Conference on
Information Security Management & Small Systems Security
September 27–28, 2001, Las Vegas, Nevada, USA

Edited by

Jan H.P. Eloff
Rand Afrikaans University
South Africa

Les Labuschagne
Rand Afrikaans University
South Africa

Rossouw von Solms
Port Elizabeth Technikon
South Africa

Gurpreet Dhillon
University of Nevada, Las Vegas
USA

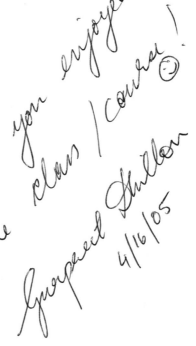

KLUWER ACADEMIC PUBLISHERS
BOSTON / DORDRECHT / LONDON

Distributors for North, Central and South America:
Kluwer Academic Publishers
101 Philip Drive
Assinippi Park
Norwell, Massachusetts 02061 USA
Telephone (781) 871-6600
Fax (781) 871-6528
E-Mail <kluwer@wkap.com>

Distributors for all other countries:
Kluwer Academic Publishers Group
Distribution Centre
Post Office Box 322
3300 AH Dordrecht, THE NETHERLANDS
Telephone 31 78 6392 392
Fax 31 78 6546 474
E-Mail <services@wkap.nl>

 Electronic Services <http://www.wkap.nl>

Library of Congress Cataloging-in-Publication Data

IFIP TC11 WG11.1/WG11.2 Working Conference on Information Security Management
& Small Systems Security (8th : 2001 : Las Vegas, Nevada)
    Advances in information security management & small systems security : IFIP TC11
WG11.1/WG11.2 Eighth Annual Working Conference on Information Security
Management & Small Systems Security, September 27-28, 2001, Las Vegas, Nevada,
USA / edited by Jan H.P. Eloff ... [et al.].
        p. cm. — (International Federation for Information Processing; 72)
    Includes bibliographical references and index.
    ISBN 0-7923-7506-8
    1. Computer security—Management—Congresses. I. Eloff, Jan H.P. II. Title. III.
International Federation for Information Processing (Series); 72.

QA76.9.A25 I465 2001
658'.0558—dc21   2001038481

Printed on acid-free paper.

Printed in the United States of America.

CONTENTS

PREFACE

The Eighth Annual Working Conference of Information Security Management and Small Systems Security, jointly presented by WG11.1 and WG11.2 of the International Federation for Information Processing (IFIP), focuses on various state-of-art concepts in the two relevant fields. The conference focuses on technical, functional as well as managerial issues.

This working conference brings together researchers and practitioners of different disciplines, organisations, and countries, to discuss the latest developments in (amongst others) information security methods, methodologies and techniques, information security management issues, risk analysis, managing information security within electronic commerce, computer crime and intrusion detection.

We are fortunate to have attracted two highly acclaimed international speakers to present invited lectures, which will set the platform for the reviewed papers. Invited speakers will talk on a broad spectrum of issues, all related to information security management and small system security issues. These talks cover new perspectives on electronic commerce, security strategies, documentation and many more.

All papers presented at this conference were **reviewed by a minimum of two international reviewers**.

We wish to express our gratitude to all authors of papers and the international referee board. We would also like to express our appreciation to the organising committee, chaired by Gurpreet Dhillon, for all their inputs and arrangements.

Finally, we would like to thank Les Labuschagne and Hein Venter for their contributions in compiling this proceeding for WG11.1 and WG 11.2.

WG11.1 (Information Security Management)
Chairman: Rossouw von Solms
E-mail: rossouw@petech.ac.za
Web address: http://www.petech.ac.za/ifip/

WG11.2 (Small Systems Security)
Chairman: Jan Eloff
E-mail: eloff@rkw.rau.ac.za
Web address: http://csweb.rau.ac.za/ifip/workgroup/

ACKNOWLEDGEMENTS

Organised by:

IFIP TC –11 Working Group 11.1 (Information Security Management)
and Working Group 11.2 (Small Systems Security)

Conference General Chair

Jan Eloff, Rand Afrikaans University, South Africa
Rossouw von Solms, Port Elizabeth Technikon, South Africa
Gurpreet Dhillon, University of Nevada, Las Vegas, USA
Les Labuschagne, Rand Afrikaans University, South Africa

Programme Committee

Jan Eloff, Rand Afrikaans University, South Africa
Les Labuschagne, Rand Afrikaans University, South Africa

Organizing Committee

Rossouw von Solms, Port Elizabeth Technikon, South Africa
Gurpreet Dhillon, University of Nevada, Las Vegas, USA

REVIEWERS

Baskerville, Richard, USA
Booysen, Hettie, South Africa
De Decker, Bart, Belgium
Deswarte, Yves, France
Dhillon, Gurpreet, USA
Drevin, Lynette, South Africa
Eloff, Jan, South Africa
Eloff, Mariki, South Africa
Girard, Pierre
Gritzalis, Dimitris, Greece
Janczewski, Lech, New Zealand
Katsikas, Sokratis, Greece
Labuschagne, Les, South Africa
Lai, Xuejia, Switserland
Oppliger, Rolf, Switserland
Preneel, Bart, Belgium
Rannenberg, Kai, UK
Smith, Elme, South Africa
Strous, Leon, The Netherlands
Teufel, Stephanie, Switzerland
Ultes-Nitsche, Ulrich, UK
Von Solms, Basie, South Africa
Von Solms, Rossouw, South Africa
Venter, Hein, South Africa
Warren, Matt, Australia
Yin, Lisa Yiqun, USA

Reviewed Papers

WEB ASSURANCE
Information Security Management for e-commerce

LES LABUSCHAGNE

RAU Standard Bank Academy for Information Technology

Rand Afrikaans University, South Africa

LL@na.rau.ac.za

Key words: Information security, e-commerce, web assurance, privacy, security services, consumer protection

Abstract: Most organisations considering the adoption of electronic commerce (EC) need to undergo a paradigm shift. The rules that usually govern business change when engaging in cyber trade. In terms of security, a similar paradigm shift needs to take place. In EC, security is no longer the protector, but has become the enabler. This article looks at what it takes to become EC-enabled and what the real security challenges are. Based on these challenges, the role of security in EC is analysed, leading to a wider view called Web assurance. Web assurance consists of three components, namely security, privacy and consumer protection. Security managers in EC-enabled organisations will have to expand their existing skills and knowledge to effectively combat the onslaught of EC.

1.   INTRODUCTION

Information security is identified by many surveys as the biggest inhibitor to electronic commerce (EC), yet when looking at security technologies, this does not seem to hold true. Many tales of horror as well as success abound, making it difficult to judge whether or not security is adequate. When a car is stolen with locked doors but open windows, it is not the security technologies that failed, but rather the ineffective or partial use thereof. Car theft, however, does not deter people from using it as a mode of transport. Its functional value outweighs its security risks.

Before attempting to evaluate the adequacy of security technologies, it is necessary to look at what makes an organisation EC-enabled. Based on these characteristics, the security challenges of EC can be defined and understood.

This article is intended to provide a framework for EC security management, based on the above-mentioned challenges, to assist a security manager in covering all the bases and, at the same time, contribute to the successful acceptance thereof. This EC security management framework is referred to as Web assurance as it encompasses more than just security [ACCE01]. EC security should not be an inhibitor of EC but rather become an enabler.

2.   WHAT ARE THE SECURITY PROBLEMS ASSOCIATED WITH ELECTRONIC COMMERCE?

Before embarking on any EC initiative, it is crucial that an organisation understands the security implications. To comprehend the security implications, the nature of EC has to be analysed. EC organisations differ substantially from one another, ranging from small retailers to large multinational corporations. Despite the differences, there are some common elements to be found in all EC organisations. There are six factors that govern an EC-enabled organisation as depicted in Figure 1 below [ROSS01]:

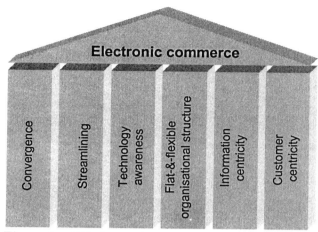

Figure 1 – EC elements

1. **Convergence** – In EC, the convergence of business and technology drives the organisation. Technology has become a business enabler and creates new business opportunities. Information technology no longer plays just a supporting role but has worked its way up into senior management circles. Most successful companies have a Chief Information Officer (CIO) on the board.

   The security challenge associated with convergence is the integration of information security architecture into the business architecture. Few business people understand information security to the extent that it is included during business strategy planning.

   Furthermore, convergence leads to EC organisations becoming totally reliant on technology, and any security breaches - unlike those in physical organisations - could lead to the demise of such an organisation. CDUniverse is an example of an EC business that had to close down after it was discovered that several credit card numbers had been stolen from it.

2. **Streamlining** – All business processes, both internal and external, must constantly be analysed for ways to make improvements. Streamlining also involves the creation of new business processes, which, in turn, might require new or additional infrastructure. Organisations can no longer function in electronic isolation of customers, partners and suppliers.

The security challenge of streamlining is the integrated nature of EC, which means that total security is no longer within the complete control of the organisation. This is especially a problem in business-to-business (B2B) EC. If a customer or supplier is negligent with passwords, no level of security is going to protect the organisation from hackers. There are many reported cases where hackers break into one organisation just to use it as a launch pad for an attack on someone else.

3. **Technology awareness** – The EC-enabled organisation must keep abreast of technological developments, as such developments create new opportunities. CEOs of the future will need a solid understanding of both the business and technological aspects affecting their organisations and industry.

   The security challenge of new technologies is that they come with new vulnerabilities. The integration of different technologies also makes it difficult to find all vulnerabilities, as it is impossible to test all possible combinations of technologies. The ever-changing environment also makes it very difficult, if not impossible, to do proper risk analysis on these systems. Employees are becoming more technologically capable and can find and exploit weak spots within systems. The abundance of hacking-related Web sites and the decline in organisational loyalty all augment the problem.

4. **Flat-and-flexible organisational structure** – The EC industry is a fast-paced one with little time for bureaucracy. The organisational structure needs to be adapted to become mobile and flexible in response to change. Employees must be empowered to make decisions and utilise opportunities. This means that the functional organisational structure of the past is inadequate and that new structures, such as project and matrix organisation structures are required.

   The security challenge with a flat-and-flexible organisational structure is that employees are now empowered to take advantage of opportunities. Less control, therefore, is possible within organisations that are having difficulty enforcing policies and procedures. Little time is spent on doing proper risk analysis before venturing into new endeavours. The balance between security and business opportunity is becoming more difficult, especially in view of point 1 above. Thus the line between accountability and responsibility becomes very hazy.

5. **Information-centricity** – EC differentiates itself from traditional commerce in the sense that information, rather than a physical product, is the primary asset. A more aggressive approach, therefore, needs to be followed for information gathering, storage and retrieval. For this purpose, more organisations are starting to use data warehousing and data mining. Information centricity also means that organisations are becoming more dependent on technology to provide the information in a timely manner.

The amount of information that has to be stored makes the security classification thereof very difficult. Access control to the information becomes problematic especially in the light of point 4 above. The availability of information is crucial to the organisation, and as such, requires well-tested disaster recovery and business continuity plans. The security issues in data warehousing – spread across several platforms – present a new area that is yet to be understood.

6. **Customer-centricity** – The focus of EC is on the individual customer, rather than on the anonymous masses. This is sometimes referred to as mass-customisation where products and services intended for the masses are packaged for the individual. Customers want to be treated as individuals, which means that organisations must get to know their customers as individuals.

To do this requires substantial private information. Possessing large amounts of private information increases the responsibility on the organisation in terms of complying with data privacy legislation. Organisations are now also more vulnerable to legal action by disgruntled clients. The socio-ethical issues in EC are unexplored and undefined territory.

The above list is by no means exhaustive but serves as a general understanding of what makes an organisation EC-enabled. The next section looks at what can be done to address some of the security problems discussed above.

3. WHAT IS ELECTRONIC COMMERCE SECURITY

Much research has been done in this field and various methods, models and approaches have been recommended. The general consensus is that EC security incorporates more that the traditional five security services of identification and authentication, authorisation, integrity, confidentiality and non-repudiation [GREE00]. EC security must address both technical and business risks if it is to be accepted. Furthermore, it must be integrated into the EC strategy, as it is an enabler for EC and not just an add-on. When comparing the security requirements for EC to those of the physical world, it becomes clear that additional requirements must be satisfied [LABU00].

In the physical world, a consumer would walk into a business and immediately make a decision on the level of trust to be placed in the organisation's transactional abilities. If it is a well-known business that has been around for some time, a trust relationship would have been built up and the consumer would not hesitate to perform transactions. The trust is further increased by the business's physical presence. The consumer has little fear that the business would disappear overnight without a trace. Talking to people face-to-face also increases the level of trust. Most consumers would also have trust in the transactional process of a physical business because, as a legal requirement, they must be audited regularly. Although irregularities might still slip through, most people feel secure in concluding transactions with physical businesses. The use of credit cards as a method of payment at restaurants, clothing shops and super-markets is common for most people.

In the realms of e-commerce, all of the above is challenged. Many new EC initiatives spring up overnight and a number of these close down just as quickly.

The lack of trust in a Web enterprise is, therefore, not unfounded, as stories of stolen credit card numbers, unfulfilled procurement and unsatisfactory products and services abound. There is no physical presence, no real people, and most importantly, no way of telling what the transactional capabilities are of the Web enterprise. This not only holds true for business-to-consumer (B2C) EC, but in some cases, also for business-to-business (B2B), business-to-government (B2G) and government-to-government (G2G) [TURB00].

Organisations wishing to engage in EC must, therefore, focus on establishing trust. One mechanism for doing this is information security. Different security mechanisms and tools can be used to provide trust in different aspects of EC, but unless a holistic approach is taken, the levels of trust will not be sufficient for clients to engage in any form of transaction [TRIA00].

Another approach is to look at Web assurance. Web assurance generally means looking at security, privacy, and consumer protection [TURB00]. Security refers to the required technology to protect transactions; privacy refers to the way in which personal information is stored and used; and consumer protection is assuring the client that the transactional processes followed are correct and that the consumer has certain recourse in the event of an unsatisfactory transaction.

Figure 2 illustrates the components making up Web assurance.

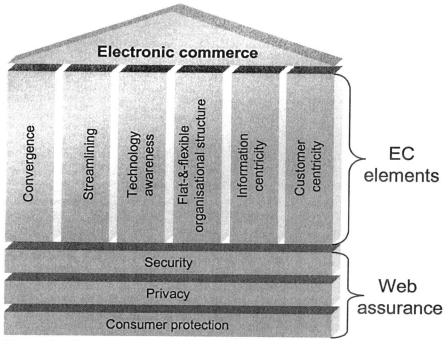

Figure 2 – Web assurance components

Following is a more detailed discussion of the Web assurance components.

3.1   Security

Different mechanisms can be used to provide the five basic security services. An additional security service that becomes very important is availability. In the realms of EC, an organisation must be able to conduct transactions 24 hours a day, 7 days a week. Business continuity planning

(BCP) and disaster recovery planning (DRP) are usually used for this purpose. Each of the 6 security services can be provided with existing technology [LABU00].

What is more important is that the client can be given the assurance that the necessary security measures are in place and being used effectively. To accomplish this, both a technical and a process assessment must be done. The technical assessment is done using penetration testing, network health checking, ethical hacking and/or configuration management auditing. Part of this assessment includes verifying if the security in the EC systems complies with the organisation's security architecture [GREE00].

The process assessment is done by verifying that the organisation complies with some baseline standards, such as the BS7799, ISO 13335, ISF or Cobit, for example [ERNS01]. Part of this assessment includes verifying whether or not the security in the EC systems complies with the organisation's security policies and procedures.

3.2   Privacy

Privacy refers to the way information is stored and retrieved within the organisation as well as how information is used by the organisation [DEPA00].

Ensuring privacy on a technical level can be achieved by means of authorisation. Not everyone needs access to all information regarding a client or transaction and the principle of least privileges can be applied. Access control can be provided through access control lists, storing the information in encrypted form and keeping logs of who accesses which information.

Also of importance is the ethical use of private information. This refers to what the organisation does with the information it has about its clients and transactions. In most cases, people would not want their private information to be given or sold to others outside the context of the original transaction. Despite legislation in many countries, spamming is still a large problem, especially for many of the free email service providers such as Hotmail and Freemail. The policy statement of the organisation determines the ethical use of private information [TURB00].

3.3 Consumer protection

Consumer protection is a concept that exists within the physical business domain as well. The main goal of consumer protection is to ensure that business is conducted in a manner that is fair to all parties involved. It is based on trust and in EC this becomes even more difficult due to its global nature. In most cases, trust can only be established through the combined use of both technical and non-technical means [TURB00].

A basic level of trust can be established by using security mechanisms such as SSL. The consumer has the assurance that all information being communicated is done so in a confidential manner, but it still provides no assurance of what the organisation is going to do with it.

An even higher level of trust can be achieved by means of non-repudiation. Non-repudiation consists of two parts, namely non-repudiation of the customer and non-repudiation of the merchant. By using digital signatures and asymmetric encryption, proof of a transaction exists that prevents any party from denying any wrongdoing. Both parties must, therefore, take responsibility for their actions and can be held accountable for any breach of contractual obligations [GREE00].

The above only provides subsequent trust in the transaction mechanism. Initial trust must first be established before a transaction will actually take place. As discussed in the introduction, initial trust is more difficult in EC. It has become necessary to find a mechanism that will establish initial trust. One mechanism that can be used for this purpose is to have the organisation and its processes audited by a trusted third party. An EC organisation can, therefore, be certified as being legitimate and following sound business principles and processes. A stamp-of-approval is given to the organisation if it complies with all the audit requirements [ARTH01].

This is becoming a prerequisite for B2B EC, as many organisations are not prepared to take the risk of dealing with 'untrusted' organisations, processes and technologies. In principle, this is similar to an organisation refusing to deal with those who do not comply with certain quality standards such as ISO 9000.

4.   CONCLUSION

Due to its particular nature, information security management for EC is becoming a specialist field. It requires a good understanding of three areas, namely security, technology and business. With EC, security cannot be treated as an afterthought or add-on as it forms part of the core of any EC initiative.

This article refers to EC security as Web assurance, based on the fact that it is more comprehensive in nature and that it is an enabler, not an inhibitor. The purpose of web assurance is to enable EC by providing clients, be they individuals, organisations or government departments, with the necessary peace of mind to make use of it. Web assurance consists, mainly, of three interwoven components namely security, privacy and consumer protection.

Security in EC should not be the limiting factor that it is currently perceived as, but should rather be viewed as an enabler.

5.   REFERENCES

[ACCE01]   Accenture, http://www.accenture.com/, eCommerce Division, 2001

[ARTH01]   Arthur Andersen, Confidence, Taking the right steps, Assurance Services, http://www.arthurandersen.com/website.nsf/content/MarketOfferingsAssurance?OpenDoc ument, 2001

[DEPA00]   Department of Communications – Republic of South Africa, Green Paper on E-Commerce, Published by the Department of Communications – Republic of South Africa 2000

[ERNS01]   Ernst & Young, Meeting Changing Information Technology Needs, Information Systems Assurance and Advisory Services, http://www.ey.com/global/gcr.nsf/ South_Africa/ZA_-_Welcome_-_ISAAS, 2001

[GREE00]   Greenstein M. & Feinman T.M., Electronic commerce — Security, Risk Management and Control, , McGraw-Hill Higher Education, ISBN 0-07-229289-X, 2000

[LABU00]   Labuschagne L., A framework for electronic commerce security, Information Security for Global Information Structures, p. 441 – 450, Kluwer Academic Press, ISBN 0-7923-7914-4, 2000

[ROSS01]   Rossudowska A., The EWEB Framework – A guideline to an enterprise-wide electronic business, Rand Afrikaans University, Masters thesis, Rand Afrikaans University Library, South Africa, 2001

[TRIA00]   Worthington-Smith, R., The E-commerce Handbook: Your guide to the Internet revolution and the future of business, Trialogue, ISBN 0-620-25915-9, 2000

[TURB00]   Turban E. et al, Electronic Commerce: A Managerial Perspective, Prentice Hall Inc., ISBN 0-13-975285-4, 2000

A MODEL AND IMPLEMENTATION GUIDELINES FOR INFORMATION SECURITY STRATEGIES IN WEB ENVIRONMENTS

C. MARGARITIS[1], N. KOLOKOTRONIS[1], P. PAPADOPOULOU[1], P. KANELLIS[2], D. MARTAKOS[1]

[1]h_margar@cc.uoa.gr, {nkolok,peggy,martakos@di.uoa.gr}
Department of Informatics and Telecommunications,
National and Kapodistrian University of Athens,
University Campus, 157 71 Athens, Greece
Tel: +3017275225
Fax: +3017275214
[2]panagiotis.kanellis@gr.arthurandersen.com
Arthur Andersen
Syngrou Ave. 377, 175 64 Athens, Greece
Tel: +3019470275
Fax: +3019425681

Keywords: Information Security Strategy, Security Semantics, Web, Systems
             Development

Abstract: The decentralised nature of web-based information systems demands a careful
             evaluation of the pantheon of security issues in order to avoid the potential
             occurrence of business risks that could not be easily mitigated. Understanding
             that information security is not merely a technical solution implemented at
             each one of the endpoints of the inter-organizational application, this paper
             presents an integrated approach based on a rigorous multi-level and multi-
             dimensional model. Through synthesis and aiming to contribute towards
             implementing the most effective security strategy possible, the approach has as
             a starting point the overall business goals and objectives. Based on those it
             aids the development of a strategy from the lower levels of securing data in
             storage and transition to the higher levels of business processes. Its use and
             applicability is demonstrated over 'Billing Mall' – a system for Electronic Bill
             Presentment and Payment.

1. INTRODUCTION

As organisations are rushing to revamp business models and align operations around e-commerce initiatives, information systems (IS) play a central role in the definition of the new value adding activities. It is without doubt that in the very near future, the largest percentage of a commercial activity will be taking place in a virtual world. Wanninger *et al.* (1997) and Papadopoulou *et al.* (2000) emphasised that such systems must be thought of as 'servicescapes' – enablers of a virtual realm where products and services exist as digital information and can be delivered through information-based channels.

The achievement of strategic goals such as increasing market share, are directly related to the reliability of the technological infrastructure of organisations. It follows that the occurrence of business risks is now more eminent as the corporate network, processes, and critical business data are vulnerable to attacks by anyone having Internet access (Abela and Sacconaghi, 1997; Derivion Corp., 1999; Segev *et al.*, 1998; Walker and Cavanaugh, 1998). What it has been observed however is that most organisations treat the Internet simply as a transport medium. The result as Segev *et al.* (1998) noted is that "...Internet security remains a relatively technical, local and distinct issue from the corporate level [IS] design and management". We advocate that, as security is the dependent variable for the success of web-based IS, the formation of any information security strategy should begin by taking into account the business vision, goals and objectives. Furthermore, it should not be approached as an afterthought, but rather it has to be designed and evolve concurrently with the development of the system. Any other way to approach this issue could result to a badly designed IS where purposive failure "...quickly leads to massive fraud, system failure, and acrimonious lawsuits" (Hughes, 1997). In summary, the definition of any effective information security strategy should thus be a well planned and concentrated effort initiated at the corporate level, and not be seen only as a local technology issue, or as an ad hoc mix of particular technical solutions to specific problems.

Taking into consideration the above issues, this paper offers an integrated approach to the development and implementation of an information security strategy for IS operating in web environments. Based on a comprehensive multi-level and multi-dimensional model, it defines the issues and sets the guidelines for infusing security both at a low and higher level. The section that follows presents the model and its building blocks for aiding the implementation of an effective security strategy. Its application is demonstrated in section 3 over a web-based Electronic Bill Presentment and Payment (EBPP) system developed for the Hellenic Telecommunications

Organisation (OTE), and currently in its deployment phase. A concluding discussion closes the article.

2. AN INFORMATION SECURITY STRATEGY MODEL

The use of security models and frameworks has been very much of a specialty area. The assumption that security is largely a technological issue and an afterthought that has to be addressed during a system's implementation phase, may explain the fact that relevant works are absent from the IS literature. However, as Baskerville (1993) notes "...a developmental duality of information systems security exists, that results because the information system and its security are treated as separate developments. This duality may cause conflict and tension between a system and its security". The model that is presented in this article was developed taking the above issue under consideration. It acquired an added importance as it was developed during our attempt to define an information security strategy for 'Billing Mall' – a system for on-line bill presentment and payment whose intended users range from corporate customers to households. Taking into account that the majority of current and potential Internet users are alert to the security issue through media over-exposure, it was clearly understood that security was a dependent variable for the level of adoption, and subsequently the future success of the system. The model which is depicted in figure 1, portrays a cyclic iterative process for designing and deploying an information security strategy depicting the different stages and successive steps that have to be taken. The stages identified, namely business needs analysis, risk analysis, security strategy implementation, and monitoring, research & analysis, are described in the rest of this section.

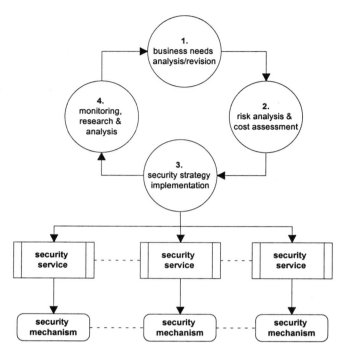

Figure 1: The life cycle of a system's security strategy

2.1 Business Needs Analysis

As already mentioned, security should be examined as an integral part of the overall strategic plan. Thus, any approach to security should start with an analysis of the business needs in order to provide a solid foundation for setting a strategy. Business Needs Analysis is the task of creating and maintaining an IS strategy that correctly reflects the overall mission and goals of the organisation. Understanding business objectives and organizational as well as inter-organizational requirements is fundamental for identifying the security requirements for a web-based IS. Since such a system may surpass the organisation's boundaries and extend across multiple organizational entities (Yang and Papazoglou, 2000), a deep understanding of business goals at strategic level is deemed necessary to enable a clear estimation of the demanded security. Some techniques that can be used for performing this task are Critical Success Factors (CSF) analysis and Strengths-Weaknesses-Opportunity-Threats (SWOT) analysis.

2.2 Risk Analysis and Cost Assessment

Since the information owned by an organisation is of critical importance, the information resources that are to be protected in terms of their value to the business goals, together with their owners and physical location should be identified. In addition, it has to be specified from whom the previously defined organizational assets should be protected from. All these issues have to be considered in conjunction with the cost of deploying the security strategy. Cost assessment will also ensure the provision of management support, an essential part for developing the strategy and a prerequisite for its future application success (Segev *et al.*, 1998). The distributed nature of web-based systems implies the existence of a multitude of vulnerabilities and threats which have to be thoroughly examined to guarantee a secure environment for commercial transactions. Potential risks should be identified at all levels of the corporate IS, including vulnerabilities and threats associated with network services, architecture, operating systems and applications.

Amongst others, typical business risks include the theft and alteration of data, unauthorised access to sensitive information, inability to meet customer needs quickly and the loss of business. Hence, the purpose of risk analysis is to facilitate decision-making about the desired level of security as well as the methods that should be adopted for preventing risks. Risk analysis can be used before the deployment of an IS to define in advance the acceptable level of risk that may be associated with it. A similar process can then be followed after deployment to re-evaluate the level of risk according to 'live' operating conditions. The difference between the acceptable risk level and the current risk level is then used as an evaluation metric. The results of the new risk analysis process can then be utilised to identify areas that require additional attention.

Risk quantification should be undertaken including a cost assessment of the possible damage associated with each threat against the cost of preventing the threat in terms of time, expenses and resources. The identified risks should then be categorised according to their probability and the severity of their impacts (see figure 2), and prioritised with respect to the cost needed for their elimination. Certainly one needs to consider first those threats resulting in greater losses (classes D and C), but still not to ignore threats of less probable financial impact, occurring more frequently (class B). Following the above steps, a complete analysis of risks is produced that can be used proactively to mitigate the number of potential threats compromising the security of an organisation's web-based IS.

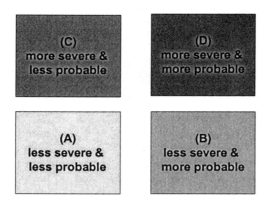

Figure 2: Risk classification

2.3 Security Strategy Implementation

When risk analysis is completed, the next step is to implement the organisation's information security strategy. The strategy should aim to ensure the most effective use of resources, and will, where appropriate constitute a consistent approach to security across a range of different systems. How the strategy is to be implemented should be described in detail in a Corporate Information Security Policy (CISP) document. Strategic objectives should be outlined. These are general security objectives, which may be defined, for instance, in terms of the levels of confidentiality, integrity, availability and accountability that the enterprise wishes to attain. The creation of the CISP is thus based upon the process of risk analysis conducted during the previous step.

2.3.1   Identifying Security Services

Undoubtedly, this is the most difficult part of the security strategy development plan, since this step involves the identification of the security services needed to be offered in order to protect the organisation's information assets from known and unknown threats (see figure 1). Not all security services are used for the protection of all kinds of information resources, since different classes of data require different levels of security. Classes of security services include integrity, confidentiality, authentication, accountability and auditing, authorisation, availability, and non-repudiation. In order to provide these security services to a web-based IS, we have to consider (a) the security mechanisms offered for data in transit, and (b) the security mechanisms offered for data in storage. These are illustrated in tables 1 and 2 respectively.

When data in transit is considered (table 1), protocols offering security services are divided into three main categories depending on the International Standards Organisation's (www.iso.ch) Open Systems Interconnection (OSI) layer they operate, namely the network, transport and the application layer. Furthermore, the application layer security mechanisms can be subdivided according to the specific structure and nature of the data they are targeting, differentiating sensitive (financial) from non-sensitive data.

Table 1: Mechanisms used to enforce the security policy for data in transit

Layer	Protection	Mechanism
network/ Internet	host-to-host	IP Security (IPSEC), IP Authentication header (AH), IP encapsulating security payload (ESP), network layer security protocol (NLSP), point-to-point tunnelling protocol (PPTP)
transport/ session	process-to-process	secure sockets layer (SSL), transport layer security (TLS), open financial exchange (OFX)
application	data structure-specific	secure hypertext transfer protocol (S-HTTP), pretty good privacy (PGP), privacy enhanced mail (PEM), secure multipurpose Internet mail extensions (S/MIME)
	data nature-specific	secure electronic transactions (SET), open financial exchange (OFX)

In general, it is easier to protect corporate assets from third parties outside the corporate network, than from its employees who intentionally or accidentally may cause severe security incidents. Thus, it is of crucial importance to ensure that everyone inside the corporate network complies with the corporate security strategy guidelines. This means that security for data in storage does not only depend on the technology used, but also on the proper administration of systems, as well as the observance of related business procedures, physical access controls, and audit functions. Not all business requirements and objectives are identical. Consequently, security mechanisms for data in storage are not absolute - there is not one standard that will fit all businesses and industries. In table 2, we present the dominant mechanisms (hardware/software based) currently available for safeguarding critical data in storage within the organisation.

Table 2: Mechanisms used to enforce the security policy for data in storage

Type		Solutions
hardware		smart cards (PVC, EMV), other tamper-proof devices, screening routers, biometric devices
software	operating system level	password-based authentication, password expiration and filtering, Kerberos-based distributed authentication, access control lists (ACL), security identifiers (SID)
	database management system level	password expiration, password standards enforcement, break-in detection and evasion, dormant user ID identification, centralised security administration, comprehensive report generation, maintenance of audit logs
	application level	anti-virus software, audit log analysers, firewalls, backup utilities

2.3.2   Defining Security Requirements at Business Process Level

Our discussion thus far has focused on the implementation of a security strategy mainly at the lower infrastructure level. We agree with Baskerville (1993) that a security strategy should evolve concurrently with the design of the system and not be approached as an afterthought. As such, any integrated approach should address how security could be possibly implemented at a higher level, i.e. the business process level. IS that support business transactions are developed based upon well-defined business process models. A business process is defined by an executive or middle manager – usually with the help of an outside consultant - and contains the following components: information flows between organizational units involved (e.g. business units, departments, agents, etc.), tasks to be performed, information sources and their usage and structure, and behaviour of all the components involved.

In order to arrive at a complete understanding of the security requirements at the business process level, Röhm *et al.* (1998) suggested examining a business transaction from at least five different perspectives/views, each one extended accordingly in order to capture the security semantics:

❑ The *business process view* representing the flow of work in terms of activities and participating entities from the viewpoint of the whole business process. It is used both as a means to communicate the architecture of the system to the stakeholders and to guide the modelling efforts for the other four viewss.

❑ The *informational view* representing the information entities, their structure and any relationships between them.

❑ The *behavioural view* showing what tasks and activities are associated with the various objects, the events that trigger these activities and the message exchanging that occurs between them.

❑ The *dynamic view* representing for each information entity all possible states and any transitions that may occur within the life cycle of the information entity.

❑ The *structural view* showing where and by whom tasks and activities are performed.

The above can guide the analyst towards acquiring a holistic view of any business process – from the highest to the lowest level. We adopt those views – placing them within the 'security strategy implementation' stage of our model and defining a hierarchy and thus the order with which they must be performed. Their practical application is demonstrated in the next section of the paper.

Most existing research in the engineering of secure information systems has used formal methods in the context of a conventional process model (Boehm, 1988). In general, a waterfall process works well for systems where requirements and design issues are well understood from the outset (Kemmerer; 1990). In the past many security critical systems exhibited these characteristics. In these environments, conventional formal methods were generally adequate. However, they are much less useful in an environment where security and other design goals may be in conflict (Baskerville, 1993). Pressures to compete against smaller or more flexible firms in global marketplaces are mounting. In response, organisations are attempting to achieve new forms that foster rapid adaptation to change. These competitive trends are forcing organisations to develop new forms of IS that are more open and adaptable to changes.

In such an environment, a multi-dimensional approach integrating security semantics with business transaction models offers significant advantages such as the following:

❑ The security ramifications of different design alternatives can be explored before the decision is made to commit to any single one.

❑ Basic verification strategy can be laid out early in the process in order to avoid the unpleasant possibility that a workable design is impossible to verify.

❑ Decisions to bypass security in order to meet other goals are made consciously early in the process, avoiding thus the possibility to be discovered as a result of a security incident much later.

2.4 Monitoring, Research and Analysis

The monitoring, research and analysis step of our model can be performed using both internal and/or external auditors. A plethora of solutions that are available widely by software vendors, such as audit log analysers and intrusion detection mechanisms can provide valuable information regarding potential implementation flaws. Their value rests on the provision of information to the administrators about the status of the systems. This information indicates possible weaknesses of the currently deployed security strategy, and may in turn constitute the starting point for radical changes in the organisation's strategic security plans and needs.

In this section we provided a comprehensive model for aiding the definition and deployment of an information security strategy from a multi-level and multi-dimensional perspective. What follows is a description of how this model was used to define and implement the security strategy of 'Billing Mall' – an EBPP system developed for the Hellenic Telecommunications Organisation (OTE).

3.   INFORMATION SECURITY STRATEGY IMPLEMENTATION

The initial response of the market to various commercial applications regarding EBPP systems is indicative of their future potential in becoming contenders for a permanent place in the worldwide Internet infrastructure. According to industry analysis, within 3-5 years the majority of bills will be presented and paid electronically (Just in Time Solutions Corp., 1999). In the United States alone it is projected that by taking the 'paper' out of the billing process, EBPP could save billers, customers and other constituents over $2 billion annually by 2002 (Ouren et al., 1998). 'Billing Mall' (http://alexandra.di.uoa.gr) is such a system, offering facilities for bill presentment and payment, customer application processing and personalised marketing (see figure 3). The system provides electronic delivery of bills to customers through the presentment of bill information in both summarised and detailed form, and secure electronic payment of a single or multiple bills upon customer request. Customer Application Processing (CAP) provides the means to customers who wish to order a new product or service that are available by OTE to do so. Finally, Personalised Marketing (PM) offers the necessary functionality and support needed for the effective promotion of products and services based on a customer's identified needs and characteristics.

The architectural model of the system is based on the Open Internet Billing (OIB) (Just in Time, 1999) model. According to OIB, a central service provider, the Consolidator, collects and stores electronic summary bills from registered billers. While offering a single point of access for viewing and paying bills, it provides the customer with the option to have access to the biller's web site for detailed bill information. When the customer visits the web site requesting to see a detailed bill, the Biller presents him with informative messages regarding products and services available. The customer is also provided with a facility for placing orders for the advertised products and/or services.

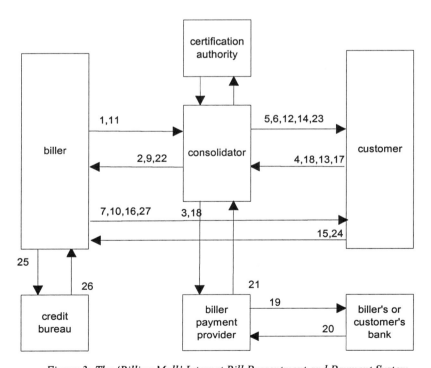

Figure 3: The 'Billing Mall' Internet Bill Presentment and Payment System

1. Biller enrols to consolidator to offer services, *2.* Biller's certificate from Certification Authority (CA), *3.* Biller Payment Provider (BPP) receives certificate from CA, *4.* Customer enrols to consolidator and selects billers, *5.* Customer's certificate from CA and login account, *6.* Announcement of new biller participating in EBPP service, *7.* New biller providing EBPP service, *8.* Request for receiving and paying bills from the new biller, *9.* Request for including the new biller in EBPP service is forwarded to biller, *10.* Notification of EBPP service becoming active for customer, *11.* Bill summary is made available to consolidator, *12.* Notification of a new bill made available for viewing and paying, *13.* Customer logs in, *14.* Bill summary is accessed by customer, *15.* Request for accessing detailed bill information, *16.* Detailed bill information and personalised marketing, *17.* Customer initiates bill payment, *18.* Payment request is forwarded to BPP, *19.* Payment execution is originated, *20.* Payment execution is completed, *21.* Notification for completion of payment, *22.* Notification for bill payment execution and remittance information, *23.* Notification for successful execution of bill payment, *24.* Order submission for biller's products and/or services, *25.* Request for information about risk of crediting customer for purchase of ordered products and services, *26.* Information about credit risk associated with customer, *27.* Notification about acceptance or rejection of submitted order.

An evaluation of the critical factors for the successful deployment and consequent adoption of the system imposed the need for the parallel development of a comprehensive security strategy. Aiming to guarantee an integrated approach to the multilateral issue of security, the model described in the previous section has served as the basis for the design and implementation of the security strategy.

Following the stages prescribed by the model, a business needs analysis has been conducted first, providing the foundation for the strategy. In this context, business goals were clearly defined, indicating the need for a system guaranteeing secure electronic transactions associated with all types of offered services. A rigorous examination of this issue denoted the security requirements that had to be satisfied in order for the system to be trusted and adopted by the intended customer base. To this end, the resources that were to be protected were identified at both organizational and inter-organizational levels, in terms of the information stored, the applications and the hardware used and the underlying network infrastructure. These corporate assets were deemed necessary to be protected from internal as well as external attacks, either intentional or accidental. Finally, in order to mitigate the cost of deploying a secure communication mechanism for financial transactions between the Consolidator and the Banks, it was decided that the existing infrastructure currently in use for fund transfer between financial institutions in Greece should be leveraged. This implied the need for including an additional entity to the OIB model, the Biller Payment Provider (see figure 3), serving as an intermediary between the Consolidator and the Banks.

The next step towards the implementation of the security strategy was to conduct a risk analysis as a proactive diagnosis of the vulnerabilities and threats that could possibly hinder the proper operation of the system. A number of entity-centric and cross-organizational risks were identified. The results of this process suggested that the potential vulnerabilities and threats should be effectively addressed by carefully selecting and applying risk prevention, detection and response methods. The analysis of revealed that the OIB model was not adequate to provide the anticipated level of security and reliability that is essential for the networked business processes. Thus, it was decided that it had to be extended in order to accommodate the establishment of a Certification Authority (CA) issuing and disseminating digital certificates to the customers (see figure 3). Furthermore, as a means for addressing the risk of insolvent customers, issuing payment transactions that could not be completed due to insufficient credit, a Credit Bureau entity was added to the architectural model of the system (see figure 3). The functional role of this entity is the provision of information related to the credit status of customers, eliminating the possibility of financial damage.

Since 'Billing Mall' requires the exchange of large amounts of financial information, the first task was to evaluate the security features of existing protocols in the field. Between Open Financial Exchange (OFX) (www.ofx.net) and Secure Electronic Transaction (SET) (www.setco.org), the former was found more appropriate mainly because (a) it is based on cryptographic protocols, (b) it supports the use of channel-level as well as application-level security, and (c) its security architecture is expandable and customisable. The SSL protocol met the requirements defined by the deliverables of the first two steps of the framework for ensuring the confidentiality and the integrity of data in transit. However, some constrains had to be put into practice concerning the cryptographic algorithms used, as well as the size of the session key. In contradiction to the OFX specification (Checkfree Corp., 1998), both server and client side certificate-based authentication is required by Billing Mall at channel-level security in order to eliminate security risks. Thus, password encryption is not required as the specification dictates for authenticating the user, who is provided with the additional capability of encrypting vital information inside the OFX message, such as credit card number and/or bank account data, with the OFX server's public key.

For this reason only one entity, satisfying the requirements imposed by the European Community's 1999/93/EC directive was decided to play the role of the certification authority. The certificates issued by the CA are based on the PKCS #6 extended-certificate syntax standard (RSA Data Security, 1993a), because of its flexibility in defining new PKCS #9 selected attribute types (RSA Data Security, 1993b) and its compatibility with applications requiring the use of X.509 certificates. In order to facilitate certificate and key management, from the customer's point of view, smart card technology was decided to be a basic part of the overall design. As far as 'Billing Mall' is concerned, a defensive policy is enforced regarding the amount for which an issued certificate can be used. This limit, which is interpreted as the amount that the user is willing to risk per transaction, is determined by the user and may be accepted or rejected by the CA and the Credit Bureau.

Firewalls, as expected, are the first line of defence for all entities (this does not include the Customer) participating in the 'Billing Mall' system. It is suggested that important information should only be accepted from and delivered to servers with a specific IP address, which means that any network package sent by an unknown IP address is automatically rejected. Example procedures taking advantage of this feature are that (a) the Consolidator only accepts bill summary information from a small set of IP addresses in the Biller's domain, and (b) the Consolidator only forwards Customer's payment requests to the specific BPP IP address. This technique allows some degree of resistance against attacks such as the 'denial of service' attack and IP spoofing.

Our aim during the design of the 'Billing Mall' was that the objectives of the information security strategy had to be integrated in the development process. Röhm *et al.* (1998) suggests that in order for this to be achieved, a business transaction must be viewed from multiple perspectives with each view extended by the security semantics of the information security strategy. In the following section we present an example of analysing the different views of the 'BILL-PAYMENT-ORDER' business process (step 17 in figure 3) and its security requirement 'non-repudiation'. In the example we use the following notation: components of existing model or attributes, which are not affected by security requirements, are described using normal text. The attributes with relevance to non-repudiation are given in bold face.

3.1 Business Process View

In electronic business transactions a document has to be signed digitally as required by the European Community's 1999/93EC Directive. A digital signature 'seals' the data to be transmitted and is created by the private key of the signatory using asymmetric cryptography. In order to study what effects a digital signature has, we will first refer to the business process view in our example. Business process modelling is typically performed in order to capture the commercially important activities. This can often lead to design conflicts once the security requirements are taken into account. In order to eliminate this tension, the supporting entities and activities that are necessary to realise the system function the way it is envisioned initially, need to be captured as well. Furthermore, since the business process view is used to guide the modelling efforts from many angles, the security semantics of the business transactions are captured in a consistent and integrated manner.

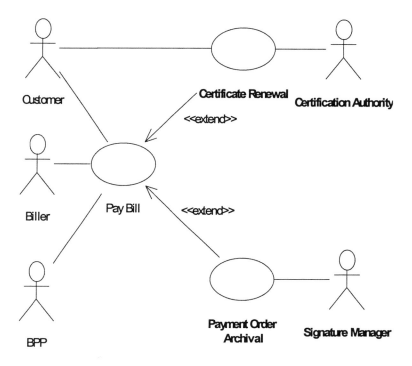

Figure 4. Business Process View extended by security semantics

Figures 4 and 5 depict graphically the 'BILL-PAYMENT-ORDER' process using Unified Modelling Language (UML) use case and activity diagrams. The use case diagram in figure 4 depicts the scenarios and actors involved in the business process of our example, while figure 5 shows the activities performed in completing the PayBill use case. In order to meet the "non-repudiation" requirement, our model has been extended by the appropriate actors (Certification Authority, Signature Manager), use cases (Certificate Renewal, Payment Order Archival) and activities (Verify Digital Signature, Verify Certificate Validity).

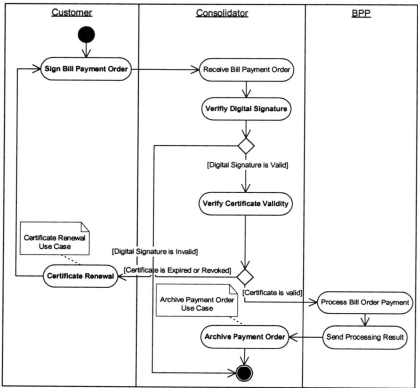

Figure 5. Activity diagram illustrating security semantics of PayBill

3.2 Informational View

According to the European Community's 1999/93/EC directive in order to sign an electronic document the 'seal' or digital signature of each signatory and the corresponding certificates are necessary. Accordingly, to effectively carry out the BILL-PAYMENT-ORDER process and to establish non-repudiation, the informational view of the transaction has to be extended by information about the signatories, the certificates used, and the trusted parties (CA) responsible for issuing the certificates. The analysis and modelling can be performed using UML class diagrams. In figure 6 we have extended the class diagram containing the customer-biller relationship of our example by appropriate classes and member fields necessary for supporting non-repudiation. These are:

❑ a new class CERTIFICATION AUTHORITY

❑ a new association class CERTIFICATE

❑ modification of the existing COMMITAL class by adding the appropriate fields for the digital signatures, and information about what algorithms were used for signing. The COMMITAL class is used to model any kind of document that should be signed by a customer (bill payment order), a biller (bill statement) or both (service level agreement).

In addition, customer and biller are specializations of a generic type signer, which must have a certificate relating the signer to a certification authority.

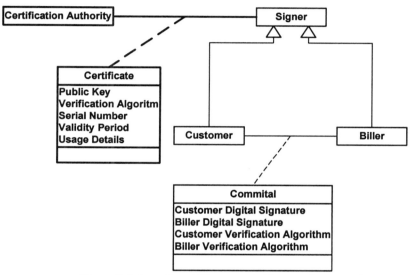

Figure 6. Informational View extended by security semantics

3.3 Behavioural View

The interactions and corresponding information flows between the entities involved in the BILL-PAYMENT-ORDER process can be analysed through the behavioural view. For the modelling of this view, UML sequence diagrams can be used. In order to assure non-repudiation, the behavioural view of the process must be modified as depicted in figure 7. The customer must digitally sign the bill payment order and the signature must be verified. In addition, because the certificate of a public key may have expired, further actions are necessary to guarantee the provability of digitally signed documents. These actions lead, for example, to extensions of the behavioural view of an object class (Verifier) responsible for validating the integrity and provability of the payment order. Again, in figure 7 necessary extensions due to security requirements are given in bold face (the sequence diagram has been enhanced by the use of scripts for accommodating complex scenarios involving conditions and iterations).

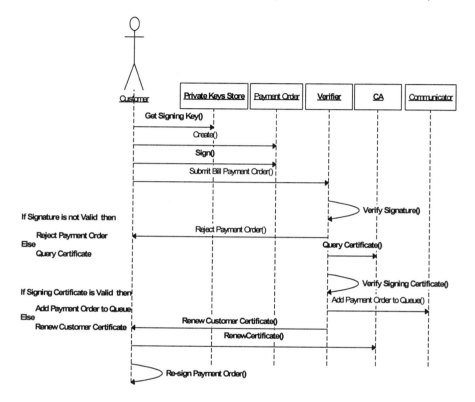

Figure 7. Behavioural View extended by security semantics

3.4 Dynamic View

The process of executing a bill payment order and establishing non-repudiation raises a number of security issues emanating from state transitions various entities undergo. These can be highlighted via an analysis and modelling of the dynamic view. In figure 8 we show the life cycle of the BILL-PAYMENT-ORDER in terms of the participating entities and their different states, using a UML state-chart diagram. As Röhm *et al.* (1998) have emphasised in a similar example, the state 'valid' is important security-wise as it represents an object of type bill payment order, which although signed, the certificate of the signatory is expired or is revoked. In this case it becomes clear that as the payment order must be re-signed.

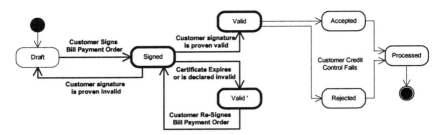

Figure 8. Dynamic View extended by security semantics

3.5 Structural View

As expected, 'non-repudiation' affects the structural view as well. Meeting critical security requirements may result in the creation and introduction of new roles with specific responsibilities. Organizational charts may need to be modified in order to mirror the new structures. In this example, a new role (Signature Manager) can be created for an employee whose main responsibility will be to check the validity of archived digital signatures, re-sign documents with certificates that are no longer valid, and monitor in general all activities in this context. Additional roles may be needed for key management (figure 9).

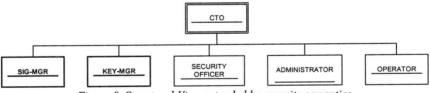

Figure 9. Structural View extended by security semantics

Using the five views for analysing and modelling the security semantics of business processes as proposed initially by Röhm *et al.* (1998), the preceding sections offer a summarised view of a single process and the security requirements that had to be infused and performed by the 'Billing Mall'. It becomes clear that by modelling and analysing the security semantics of the business transactions it supports, the IS and its security are not treated as separate developments. As the former becomes part of the design process, the possible duality as a cause for conflict (Baskerville, 1993) is eliminated.

4. CONCLUSIONS

In this article we presented an integrated approach for the development of an information security strategy based on a rigorous multi-level and multi-dimensional model. The position that any security strategy must evolve concurrently with the design of the system and not be approached as an afterthought is reflected in the model, which (a) monitors closely the development phases of an IS, and (b) addresses security at the business process level. Enabling the practitioner to evaluate and use the available security tools and techniques in a consistent manner, the structure of the model enforces the view that any security strategy must be conducted primarily at a higher level, and not be seen merely as a local technology issue. Without doubt we believe that the approach presented herein could be further refined and enhanced. We hope that its further adoption will result to any necessary enhancements or modifications, incrementing thus its value regarding its practical applicability. 'Waterproof' security of large inter-organizational systems is an issue of immense complexity, but we believe that we have at least made a few but necessary steps towards meeting this challenge.

ACKNOWLEDGEMENTS

We gratefully acknowledge the *Greek Secretariat for Research and Technology (GSRT)* for financing the 'Billing Mall' project. We would also like to thank the partners involved in the project: Athens University of Economics and Business, Cyberce, Datamedia, Dias, Sysware, Teiresias and the University of Crete.

REFERENCES

ABELA, A and J.R SACCONAGHI (1997). Value exchange: The secret of building customer relationships on line. *The McKinsey Quarterly* , 2, 216 –219.

BASKERVILLE, R. (1993). Information Systems Security Design Methods: Implications for Information Systems Development, *ACM Computing Surveys*, 25(4), 375-414

BOEHM, B. (1988), A Spiral Model of Software Development, *IEEE Computer*, May, pp 61-72.

CHECKFREE Corp., INTUIT Inc. and MICROSOFT Corp. (1998) *Open Financial Exchange*. Specification 1.5.1.

DERIVION Corp. (1999). Internet Billing and the Mid-Tier Biller: Enjoying the Benefits of Electronic Bill Presentment and Payment without Operational Compromise. Available at http://www.derivion.com/index 9.html

HUGHES, E. (1997). A long-term perspective on electronic commerce. *Networker*, Nov/Dec, 38 –50.

JUST IN TIME SOLUTIONS Corp. (1999). The Value of Internet Billing. Available at http://www.justintime.com/internetbilling/index.html

KEMMERER, R. A. (1990), Integrating Formal Methods into the Development Process, *IEEE Software*, Sep, 37-50

OUREN, J., M. SINGER, J. STEPHENSON and A. L. WEINBERG (1998). Electronic bill presentment and payment. *The McKinsey Quarterly*, 4, 98 –106.

PAPADOPOULOU, P., A. TRIANTAFILLAKIS, P. KANELLIS and D. MARTAKOS (2000). A generic framework for the deployment of an Internet billing servicescape. In *Proceedings of the 1st World Congress of Electronic Commerce*, Hamilton, Ontario, Canada, January 19-21.

RÖHM, A.W., PERNUL, G. and HERRMANN, G. (1998). Modelling secure and fair electronic commerce. In *Proceedings of the 14th Annual Computer Security Applications Conference*, Scottsdale, AZ., Dec. 7-11, IEEE Computer Society Press.

RSA DATA SECURITY Inc. (1993). *PKCS #6: Extended –Certificate Syntax Standard*, version 1.5.

RSA DATA SECURITY Inc. (1993). *PKCS #9: Selected Attribute Types*, version 1.1.

SEGEV, A., J. PORRA and M. ROLDAN (1998). Internet security and the case of bank of America. *Communications of the ACM*, 41, Oct, 81 –87.

WALKER, K.M. and L.C. CAVANAUGH (1998). *Computer security policies and SunScreen firewalls*. Sun Microsystems Press.

WANNINGER, L., C. ANDERSON and R. HANSEN (1997). Designing Servicescapes for Electronic Commerce: An Evolutionary Approach. Available at http://www.misrc.umn.edu/wpaper/default.asp

YANG, J. and PAPAZOGLOU, M.P. (2000). Interoperation Support for Electronic Business. Communications of the ACM, 43, June, 39-47.

A THREE-DIMENSIONAL FRAMEWORK FOR SECURITY IMPLEMENTATION IN MOBILE ENVIRONMENTS

BETHUEL ROBERTO VINAJA

Department of Computer Information Systems and Q.M., College of Business Administration, University of Texas Pan American, Email: vinajar@panam.edu

Abstract: This paper describes a framework that can be used to identify security requirements for a specific mobile environment. The model includes three dimensions: mobile users, mobile hardware and mobile software. The analysis of the three dimensions can determine the characteristics of the specific implementation and needed security measures. Specific security measures for mobile hardware, mobile users and mobile software are also discussed.

Key words: Security, Mobility, Mobile Agents, Mobile Computers, Wireless

1.   INTRODUCTION

The concept of mobility has become prevalent as the adoption of the Internet and wireless devices continues to grow. Strategy Analytic predicts that by 2004 there will be over one billion wireless device users and approximately 600 million wireless Internet subscribers. In this paper, we will examine the security aspects of mobility using a three-dimensional framework that analyses mobility in three aspects: mobile code, mobile hardware and mobile users. This framework distinguishes between three categories of mobility: hardware mobility, software mobility and user mobility.

2.   MOBILE HARDWARE

Most transactions are still conducted at fixed locations using fixed personal computers and fixed terminals. Mobile devices provide users with convenient flexibility to conduct transactions and access information from multiple and varied locations, without being tied to any specific physical location. However, mobile devices have some limitations too. Most wireless networks and satellite-based systems have limited bandwidth. Cellular phone and satellite-based connections are generally more expensive than regular phone lines and ISDN. Given the bandwidth and cost challenges, it is very inefficient to handle long sessions and transfer large amount of data by using mobile devices (Wang et. al.1998). According to Chen (2000), the current network platforms have repeated shifts in both topology and network conditions. Such volatility in topology is attributed to:

1. Changes in the availability of various intermediate network hosts.
2. Mobility of mobile hosts such as laptops.
3. General shifts in network usage patterns that may affect bandwidth and host availability.

3.   MOBILE USERS

Users are no longer accessing resources from a fixed location. Chen (2000) points out two possible scenarios:

- The user is relatively stationary towards a mobile device. A mobile user is one who accesses the Internet by using a laptop or portable computer.
- The user is mobile in relation to access devices. This user is called nomadic. A nomadic user accesses the Internet, but might move from one terminal to another.

The Internet open architecture allows resource sharing for both mobile and nomadic users. We can expect that as the Internet continues to spread out, more and more users will be classified as either mobile or nomadic. Both mobile and nomadic users need to transparently access resources either from a portable computer or any terminal connected to the Internet.

4.   MOBILE SOFTWARE

Mobile computing has been already very successful, and mobile agents are now revealing that software can also be mobile. Mobile agent technology implies moving active code over spatially different places. An agent is a software program that can autonomously perform a task on behalf of its user. Systems may combine static agents with mobile agents (Kearney 1998). The mobile agent paradigm encompasses three areas: Artificial Intelligence, networking, and operating systems. (Vogler et. al. 1998). From the Artificial Intelligence viewpoint, mobile agents are defined as autonomous software. From the operating system viewpoint, mobile agents are an evolution of code migration. Finally, from the networking viewpoint, mobile agents are an extension of client/server computing.

Mobile agents have several advantages. For example, mobile agents are relatively more efficient than traditional software programs and consume fewer network resources, because the agent moves the computation to the data, rather than the data to the computation. An additional characteristic is fault tolerance, that is mobile agents do not require a continuous network connection. An agent can start a job, disconnect, and later reconnect and get the results. Many mobile agents are implemented as Java applications. One of the advantages of Java applications is that they can be accessed from any terminal with Internet access. The requirements for executing an applet (Java application) are minimum; only a Java-enabled browser is required, and most popular browsers are Java-enabled. The following are some sample mobile agent applications.

One of the first mobile agent systems was Telescript, developed by General Magic, which by means of mobile agents, enables automated as well as interactive access to a network of computers.

D'Agents is a mobile agent designed at Dartmouth that supports mobile computers and disconnected operation. It is equipped with network-sensing tools and a docking system that allows the agent to transparently move between mobile computers, regardless of when the computers connect to a network (Brewington et. al. 1999).

Mobiware is an adaptive mobile networking environment based on distributed object technology. Built on CORBA and Java, it runs on mobile devices, wireless access points and mobile-capable switch/routers providing a set of open interfaces for adaptive mobile networking.

5. THE THREE-DIMENSIONAL FRAMEWORK

Dix et. al. 2000 have proposed a useful framework that can be used as a tool for the design of interactive mobile systems. The framework consists of taxonomies of location, mobility, population, and device awareness. The mobility dimension classifies levels of hardware mobility within the environment into three main categories:

—fixed: that is, the device is not mobile at all (e.g., a work station fixed in a particular place)
—mobile: may be moved by others (e.g., a PDA or computer that is carried around)
—autonomous: may move under its own control (e.g., a robot).

The taxonomy proposed by Dix, is very useful, but mobility is described using only one dimension, the hardware dimension. We can expand the analytical power of the framework by adding the software dimension and the user dimension. Our proposed framework is a three-dimensional matrix with three axis: mobile/static computers, mobile/static software and mobile/static users (Figure 1). Different applications can be differentiated in this basic classification matrix based on the criteria of computers, software and users. This framework can be used to categorise existing environments and even future developments. We can assign different scenarios to a three-dimensional space. Complete applications can be assigned to the areas of the matrix.

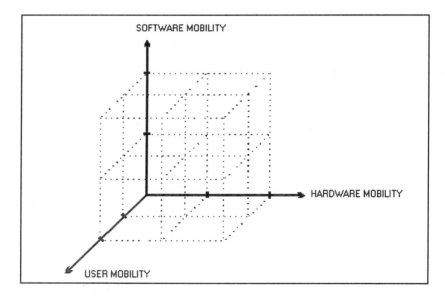

Figure 1. Three-dimensional framework

Personal computers, mainframes and computing centres are example of static computing environments. Laptops, PDAs, and cellular phones are examples of mobile environments. In a pure mobility environment all three dimensions (user, hardware and software) are mobile. This is represented as the upper front cube. The lower-back cube represents traditional fixed environments. Other cubes include a mix of mobile and static characteristics. Table 1 describes sample scenarios combining the three dimensions.

Table 1. Sample environments

Hardware	Software	User	Scenario
Static	Static	Static	A PC user at home.
Static	Static	Mobile	A user at the computer centre.
Static	Mobile	Static	A user launching Mobile agents at the computer centre
Static	Mobile	Mobile	A user launching agent from several static computers
Mobile	Static	Mobile	A salesperson using a laptop with office software.
Mobile	Mobile	Mobile	The optimum configuration

Some of the quadrants in our three-dimensional space are difficult situations to define. In fact, the combination static user and mobile hardware is paradoxical, a static user, which always remains at the exact same location, would not get any value-added benefit from using a laptop or PDA. There may not be a real life situation that fits into some categories. However, these "empty" quadrants may present new opportunities to be discovered or new combinations of mobility dimensions.

The following is an example of the application of the framework to a specific scenario. The results are then interpreted and appropriate security measures are suggested. For example, a combination mobile hardware and mobile software for a mobile user would represent a pure mobile environment (Figure 2).

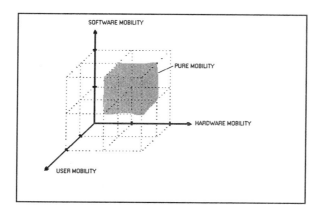

Figure 2. Pure mobility scenario

First, we analyse the hardware dimension. In our sample scenario a laptop is used. The laptop is more likely to get lost or stolen than a fixed computer because it is smaller and handy. If the laptop gets lost, the data on it gets lost too. If a third party steals or finds the laptop, that person might get unauthorised access to corporate resources. The proposed solution is the user of strict authentication protocols so that the laptop can be used only by its owner, and not by anybody in possession of it.

Second, we analyse the software dimension. In our sample scenario, the user is launching mobile agent applications. The security implications are that the agent can be denied access by some server firewalls or filters. The solution to this problem can be to provide some cross-platform agent authentication mechanism so the server can verify the agent is coming from a trusted source. In those cases where the agent opens its code and data to the host server, there is the possibility for a malicious host server to modify this code and alter the agent behaviour. The solution to this security issue could be a partial or selective release of source code depending on the level of trust of the host server. Another solution could be to provide the agent with an "auto-disable" function in the event its source code is modified at the host server.

Finally, we analyse the user dimension. In our hypothetical case, the user is also mobile. A nomadic user, which is accessing the corporate network from multiple locations, requires some form of authentication in order to validate his/her identity. The main security concern in the user dimension is how to provide proper authentication. Passwords are the easier method of authentication, however mobile users might access the network from multiple locations and accidentally leave an open session. Another person might use the same computer and find the open session, and consequently an open door to confidential corporate data. A solution can be the use of other authentication methods based on smart cards or token authentication. However, the smart card can be lost too. A better solution can be the use of biometric authentication. Biometric methods can authenticate based on who the person is (unique characteristics), instead of what the person has (smart card method) or what the person knows (password method).

6.   SECURITY IN A MOBILE ENVIRONMENT

Mobile devices and especially wireless devices require additional and more sophisticated security methods. Mobile devices are particularly exposed to specific risks not encountered in static environments. Mobile systems break assumptions that are implied in the design of fixed-location computer applications. Wireless devices always carry some level of uncertainty. Some of the potential risks include altered information, denial of access, interrupted transactions, transmission delays and power outages, (Davies 1994). In the case of a PDA used for electronic signatures, the user would need to always carry the PDA. If the device is left out of sight for even a few moments, somebody might modify the signing program. The smart card could be stolen or modified too (Freudenthal et. al. 2000).

Mobile computers and wireless devices could also become the preferred tool for hackers given the difficulty to determine where an attack is coming from. Mobile devices are not linked to any specific geographic location, and the attacker can quickly get on-line or off-line, so it would be more difficult to determine the location of the hacker. As Chess (1998) states: "When a program attempts some action, we may be unable to identify a person to whom that action can be attributed, and it is not safe to assume that any particular person intends the action to be taken".

Malicious mobile scripts represent a significant risk for wireless devices. The potential damages of viruses, which are very well known in traditional fixed environments, can be even more malicious in a mobile environment. As one user moves from one cell area to the next, there is a security hole during the handing off process. It is during this lapse of time, that attackers can distribute malicious code and cause denial of service (Ghosh and Swaminatha 2000). In a traditional fixed environment, hackers break into a computer system; the attacker 'comes' to the targeted computer. In the case of wireless Internet access, the hacker can passively wait for its prey, which becomes an easy target as the user roams into the attacker's zone. The victim falls into the prepared 'trap'.

The authentication method used in mobile devices it is also an Achilles' heel. Many mobile devices authenticate only at initial connection. If connection is lost due to intermittent service failures and unreliable conditions (which is very usual with wireless devices,) the connection is re-established without re-authenticating. At this time, the reconnected session is not protected and a hacker can easily introduce viruses along with the transmitted data (Ghosh and Swaminatha 2000).

Users are commonly reluctant to transmit credit card information over the Internet, because they are concerned that their private information might be stolen or misused. This risk is even greater in the case of mobile Internet access. Lack of transaction security in mobile devices can be a major impediment for the adoption of M-Commerce. Ghosh and Swaminatha (2000) suggest the following security requirements to address the special risks of mobile computers/devices:

- Memory protection for processes
- Protected kernel rings
- File access control
- Authentication of principals to resources
- Differentiated user and process privileges
- Sandboxes for untrusted code
- Biometric authentication.

Mobile devices or agents could be used for transferring controlled technologies and violate existing export regulations. Mobile agents and devices navigate from one location to another, making enforcement of export regulations more difficult (Bohm, Brown and Gladman 2000). Given all existing barriers on the export of intangibles, people may try to circumvent controls by using mobile devices agents, try to embedded encryption technology inside an intelligent agent, or as part of a mobile device.

7.   FUTURE RESEARCH ISSUES

There are many opportunities for future research in the mobile security field. Current security protocols for mobile devices are alarmingly simple. A major limitation of mobile devices is its narrow bandwidth and capacity. This restraint forces designers to give up security and encryption to simplify the process and therefore improve on-line performance. Existing protocols for wireless devices are not as powerful as fixed-computer protocols. Clearly, there is a need for a protocol that is both efficient and powerful.

Future mobile applications might provide the ability to use e-cash stored on a phone's smartcard for purchases. The use of mobile devices for electronic payments can introduce additional security concerns. Malicious scripts might be able to off-load money from smartcards. The environment for conducting e-commerce transaction using a mobile device should support the following features (Van Thanh 2000):

- User authentication
- Merchant authentication
- Secure (encrypted) channel
- User friendly payment scheme supporting micropayments
- Receipt delivery
- Simple user interface.

Transaction security protocols such as SET are not suitable for wireless devices because of its complexity and resource requirements. More research is needed in the area of transaction security protocol for mobile devices.

8.   CONCLUSION

This paper has described a proposed framework that can be used to identify security requirements for a specific mobile environment. The model includes three dimensions mobile users, mobile hardware and mobile software. Based on the combinations of these three dimensions we can determine the characteristics of the specific implementation and suggest needed security measures. Mobile agent technologies and mobile computers will play an important role in the future, however many security issues need to be addressed before the technology can be fully implemented.

9. REFERENCES

Bohm, Nicholas, Brown, Ian and Gladman, Brian, "Strategic Export Controls: The Impact on Cryptography," *The Foundation for Information Policy Research*, Available online at: www.fipr.org

Brewington, Brian, Gray, Robert, Moizumi, Katsuhiro, Kotz, David, Cybenko, George and Rus, Daniela, "Mobile Agents for Distributed Information Retrieval," In Klusch, Mathias (Ed.): *Intelligent Information Agents*, Springer-Verlag, Germany, 1999, pp. 354-395

Chen, Larry T., "AgentOS: The Agent-based Distributed Operating System for Mobile Networks."

Davies, N., Blair, G., Cheverst, K., And Friday, A., "Supporting Adaptive Services in a Heterogeneous Mobile Environment," *In Proceedings of the Workshop on Mobile Computing Systems and Applications* (Mobile '94, Santa Cruz, CA, Dec.), IEEE, Los Alamitos, CA, 153–157.

Freudenthal, Margus, Heiberg, Sven and Willemson, Jan, "Personal Security Environment on Palm PDA," *IEEE*, 2000.

Ghosh, Anup K. and Swaminatha, Tara M., "Software Security and Privacy Risks in Mobile E-Commerce, *Communications Of The ACM*, February 2001, Vol.44, No.2.

Kearney, P., "Personal Agents: A Walk on the Client Side", In: Jennings, N.R. and Wooldridge, M.J., *Agent Technology*, Springer-Verlag, Germany, 1998, pp. 125-136.

Romao, Artur and Mira Da Silva, Miguel, "An Agent-Based Secure Internet Payment System for Mobile Computing," *Proceeding of Trends in Distributed Systems 1998: Electronic Commerce,* Hamburg, Germany, LNCS, Springer-Verlag, June 3-5, 1998.

Van Thanh, DO, "Security Issues in Mobile eCommerce," *IEEE*, 2000.

Vogler, Hartmut, Moschgath, Marie-Luise and Kunkelman, Thomas, "Enhancing Mobile Agents with Electronic Commerce Capabilities," In Klusch, Matthias and Weib, Gerhard, *Cooperative Information Agents II, Proceedings of the Second International Workshop, CIA 1998*, Paris France, July 1998, Springer-Verlag, Germany, pp. 148-159.

Wang, X.F., Lam, K.Y. and Yi, X., "Secure Agent-Mediated Mobile Payment," In Ishida, Toru (ed.) *Multiagent Platforms, First Pacific Rim International Workshop on Multi-Agents, PRIMA 98*, Singapore, November 1998, LNCS 1599, Springer-Verlag, Germany, pp.162-173.

MAINTAINING INTEGRITY WITHIN MOBILE SELF PROTECTING OBJECTS

Wesley Brandi

Department of Computer Science, Rand Afrikaans University
PO Box 524, Auckland Park, Johannesburg, 2006 South Africa
wb@eclab.rau.ac.za

Martin S Olivier

Department of Computer Science, Rand Afrikaans University
PO Box 524, Auckland Park, Johannesburg, 2006 South Africa
molivier@rkw.rau.ac.za

Abstract   This paper examines the integrity issues involved when a Self Protecting Object (SPO) is moved to a site in a federated database which will eventually disconnect and become unreachable for some time. The SPO model guarantees that the custom security policy of a site participating in a federated database will be implemented and respected when the object it shares is accessed by others in the federated database, regardless of the objects location.

We introduce the Mobile Self Protecting Object (MSPO) and propose an architecture within which it will operate. Having looked at integrity issues which may arise we propose a way in which to maintain integrity within Mobile Self Protecting Objects. In particular, we propose a way in which to deal with mobile transactions which require authorisation. We discuss how MPSOs can be updated whilst in a mobile environment as well as how to ensure an MSPO has maintained its integrity upon re-entering the federated database from a mobile site.

Keywords: Mobile self protecting object, federated database, integrity, security

1.   INTRODUCTION

The demand for access to information in a database from a mobile environment is steadily increasing [TIP00]. This trend is applicable to clients in a federated database requesting access to a Self Protecting Object (SPO) from some form of mobile media. The SPO model proposed by [OLI96] allows objects in a federated database to move from their originating site to a trusted remote site in the federated database whilst guaranteeing that the originating site's security policy will be implemented.

It may not suffice to merely have access to an SPO through the federated database from a mobile environment since the need may arise to access an SPO when access to the federated database is not feasible. This demand gives rise to a new form of SPO, the Mobile Self Protecting Object (MSPO).

An MSPO can be defined as an SPO that has been relocated from a site in the federated database to a mobile site for the exclusive use of the mobile user of that site upon disconnection. [BAD95] refers to such clients (sites) as *hoard clients*.

We define integrity within SPOs as a means of ensuring the validity of an SPO within a federated database environment. When we now consider integrity within MSPOs, the definition of integrity remains, but the way in which the integrity of an MSPO is maintained differs. When an MSPO is once again returned to the federated database from the mobile media on which it was previously located, how can one be certain that the MSPO has maintained its integrity? The aim of this paper is to provide and define a framework for the MSPO concept as well as to examine how integrity within MSPOs can be maintained and implemented.

In section 2 we briefly discuss the SPO architecture and the framework within which it operates. Before we discuss how integrity within the MSPO architecture can be implemented we first propose a model for the MSPO architecture. This is covered in section 3. We then examine how integrity can be implemented and maintained in section 4. The paper is concluded in section 5.

2. BACKGROUND

We follow The SPO model proposed by [OLI96]. It is an object-oriented model implemented within a federated database architecture. A federated database is a distributed database [CP85] where participating sites (database systems) are fairly autonomous. See [SL90] for a thorough discussion of federated databases. A federated database defines a general security policy which is implemented by all participating sites. The SPO model takes this further in that each site, having implemented the federated security policy, extends it to include their own security policy. It is assumed that this security policy will be respected and implemented by other sites when accessing data on that site.

This model therefore allows objects originating at one site to be relocated to another, ensuring that the security policy of the originating site will be implemented. Each site in the federated database must implement a core layer of the SPO model, this core is referred to as the Trusted Common Core (TCC), this core is responsible for ensuring that each site's security policy is maintained. In addition to this, code can be appended to objects in the form of a Trusted Extension (TE). This module is a form of a portable security policy specific to the object it is embedded in. In order for the TE of an object to function correctly, a Trusted Local Extension (TLE) is included at each site in the federated database, it provides any support required by the TE.

3.   MSPO ARCHITECTURE

We define an MSPO as an SPO that has been transferred into a mobile environment and subsequently removed from the federated database. Before an SPO can be made mobile, the site requesting the transfer must be authorised to do so by the TLE of the site where the SPO originated from. The TLE of the original site will receive a request to make the SPO mobile. The request is much like that of a normal transfer request, in that an SPO is being moved from site A to site C. It differs only in that site C belongs to its parent site B, and site C will eventually disconnect itself from its parent site and therefore from the federated database. Site C is therefore a mobile site within the member site B.

3.1.   MOBILE SITES

[OLI97] proposes a model for mobiles nodes (sites) in a federated database. This model has each site hosting a mobile site implement a modified TCC, referred to as an HTCC (host TCC). Each mobile site then implements a Mobile Trusted Core, which essentially mirrors the HTCC. SPOs moved from a federated site to a mobile site are modified prior to their relocation. In being modified, the object will not include any methods or variables that the mobile site will not be authorised to use. This implies that once an SPO has been relocated to the mobile site, no authorisation will be necessary to use it.

We propose an alternative approach to the mobile architecture; we assume that an SPO will not be used at all if it is not accessed through the TCC. One can argue that modifying an SPO does not necessarily address the problem of security in our model, since although an SPO will be secure once modified and copied to a mobile site. This is not the case when relocating an SPO to a normal site in the federated database, since SPOs relocated to these sites will not be modified.

A mobile site in our proposed model is much like that of a site which is a member of a federated database. The mobile site is slightly different in that it is a child site to a parent site which in turn is an official member site of the federated database. Some degree of authentication must exist between the mobile child site and its parent site, thus minimising the risk of an intruder masquerading as the mobile child site.

A mobile site must implement and trust the TCC, therefore as is the case with member sites of the federated database, a mobile site can only use an SPO through the TCC. This level of trust is essential. An SPO can not be moved to a site where the TCC is not trusted or is not implemented completely. In our proposed model, a mobile site can only have one parent site and can only connect to the federated database via this parent site. Figure 1 illustrates the mobile site architecture.

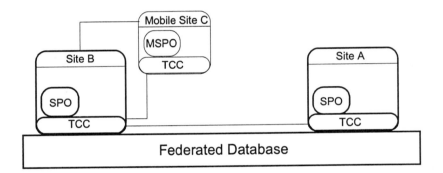

Figure 1   The mobile site model

3.2.   RELOCATION

Relocating an SPO to a mobile site is similar to the transfer process of an SPO. Since a mobile site is not a complete member of the federated database, it will have its parent site make the request it's behalf. As is the case with transfer requests of an SPO in a federated database, the request to move an SPO to a mobile site must be authorised. When moving an SPO to a mobile site, authorisation must be gained from the SPO's originating site.

A request to move an SPO from site A to site C, assuming site C is a mobile site belonging to site B, would have the TCC include this information in its request to the TLE of the SPOs home site. Upon authorisation, the TLE will then perform several tasks which are essential to maintaining the integrity of the soon to be MSPO:

- Keep record that the SPO has been moved to the mobile site C, a child site of the member site B.

- Create a duplicate of the SPO and save it locally.

- Create and store hashes of all the values in the SPO that require authorisation to be modified.

- Create and store a hash of the entire SPO.

If the mobile site that an SPO has been relocated to is still active, in that it has not yet been disconnected from the federated database, the SPO can still be used normally, since the TCC of the mobile site is similar to a TCC of a participating site in the federated database.

3.3.   REMOVAL FROM THE FEDERATED DATABASE

The fact that a site is mobile means that it will eventually become unavailable, in that it will disconnect itself from the federated database. Before a mobile site can disconnect from the federated database (its parent site), it must request authorisation from its parent site. If an MSPO that the mobile site is hosting is currently in use, the request to disconnect the site will be denied. Once the request has been authorised, the mobile site is then free to disconnect. The parent site will then inform the originating sites of the MSPOs hosted by the mobile site that the MSPOs have been disconnected from the federated database.

Having been disconnected from the database, an SPO is no longer available for modification in the federated database until it has been reintroduced into the system. However, if necessary, it is possible for sites to retrieve data from the duplicated SPOs as long as the sites retrieving the data understand that the SPOs are currently active elsewhere, hence, the data may not be valid. We do not analyse the concurrency issues involved when an SPO becomes mobile and is disconnected from the federated database; this is not within the scope of this paper and will be covered in future research.

Upon disconnection of a mobile site from the federated database, a timer on the parent site will be associated with the length of time of that the mobile site has been disconnected. If the timer exceeds a predefined threshold, the mobile site and the MSPOs it was hosting will be considered lost and the duplicate SPOs will be introduced into the federated database from the SPOs respective original sites.

This rollback policy will ensure that any MSPO that has been lost while disconnected from the federated database will be reintroduced into the database in its most recent consistent state.

Since a mobile site may disconnect without prior warning, and therefore without authorisation, a site hosting the mobile site must be able to handle such situations effectively. The primary reason for a mobile site to obtain authorisation before disconnecting is to accommodate any transactions that may be running on any of the MSPOs it is currently hosting. The worst case scenario in such a situation may be that a transaction does not run to completion. This transaction would have to be aborted, the parent site would then begin the process of handling the mobile site disconnection, as described earlier.

4. MAINTAINING INTEGRITY OF AN MSPO

The proposed MSPO architecture of the previous section gives us a framework in which to now examine and discuss methods as to how the integrity of an MSPO can be maintained. We believe that there are three major issues, that when addressed and implemented in a proper manner, will ensure integrity within the MSPO architecture. The issues we have identified are the following:

- The proper management of transactions in a mobile environment that require authorisation.

- An orderly and secure manner in which to update MSPOs.

- A process of re-entry for an MSPO into the federated database.

We begin this discussion by looking at general functionality of an MSPO and move onto an analysis of how transactions which require authorisation are dealt with whilst the mobile site is disconnected. We will then discuss how an MSPO can be updated and examine the process involved when an MSPO is to re-enter the federated database.

4.1. MSPO FUNCTIONALITY OUTSIDE OF THE FEDERATED DATABASE

Since the site an MSPO is hosted on is mobile, upon disconnection the TCC associated with that site may have no means of making contact with any other sites of the federated database. This has an impact particularly on transactions which require some kind of interaction with the TLE of an MSPO's originating site. Since the TCC may have no way of establishing contact with any member sites of the federated database, transactions which require authorisation or some kind of interaction with the MSPO's originating site may be denied execution by the TCC.

In light of this problem, before a transaction will be allowed to execute within a mobile site, the TCC will first analyse the nature of the transaction. From this, the TCC will determine what (if any) authorisation requirements there are for the transaction and whether or not the authorisation may be attained.

It could be the case that a mobile site may be able to establish contact with its parent site via a cellular link or remote network, thereby allowing the TCC to communicate with other sites of the federated database and attain proper authorisation for transactions. On the other hand, it may be the case that the mobile site may not be able to establish contact with its parent site, any transactions requiring authorisation will therefore be denied permission to execute.

Figure 2 illustrates the flow of operations as a transaction which requires authorisation from a site on the federated database attempts to execute.

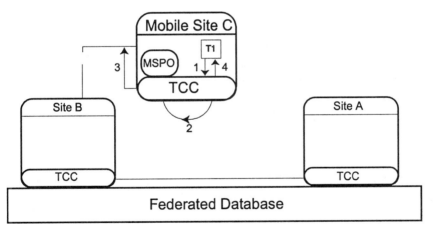

1. Request to execute transaction 'T1'.
2. The TCC analyses the nature of transaction T1 and determines authorisation from site A is required.
3. The TCC attempts to establish a connection to its parent, site B.
4. Since the TCC can not establish a connection to site B, transaction T1 is denied permission to execute.

Figure 2 An illustration of the steps taken by a mobile site to establish a connection for a transaction requiring authorisation.

Since an MSPO can only be used within the framework of a trusted TCC on a mobile site, and since transactions which require authorisation will only be executed provided that the TCC of the mobile site can establish contact with its parent site, we can be assured that the integrity of the MSPO will not be maliciously compromised whilst it is disconnected from the federated database.

The integrity of each MSPO is still subject to several forms of compromise the likes of errors, viruses or failures in the system [CFM95]. Section 4.4 discusses how such compromises are detected and what action is taken upon detection.

4.2.   EXECUTING TRANSACTIONS WHICH REQUIRE AUTHORISATION

If the TCC of a mobile site is able to establish contact with its parent site, it can begin the process of obtaining authorisation for the transaction to be executed within the mobile site on an MSPO. Having obtained authorisation the transaction will execute and run to completion. Upon completion of the transaction, steps similar to those performed on an SPO will be taken in order to maintain the integrity of the MSPO: A duplicate of the MSPO will be made and sent to its originating site where a hash of the MSPO as well of each value that requires authorisation to be modified will be created and stored.

As an example of executing transactions on mobile sites which require authorisation, consider a car salesman who has moved an SPO of type Car onto his laptop. He is currently at a client's premises and the client has requested details on the lifetime of the gear box. The salesman queries the gear box lifetime property of the Car MSPO and is subsequently requested to connect to the federated database. The gear box lifetime property is a property which requires authorisation in order to be read. The TCC on the salesman's laptop observed the nature of the salesman's query and identified the need for authorisation, hence, the salesman has been prompted to connect to the federated database.

Should the salesman not connect to the database, the TCC will be unable to obtain authorisation and the query to view the gearbox lifetime property will be denied. If the salesman does connect the laptop to the federated database, he may be prompted for a username and password, upon successful authorisation the TCC will grant permission to run the query and hence view the gearbox lifetime property.

We have so far assumed that should a mobile site be unable to establish a connection to its parent site, any transactions that require authorisation will simply be denied permission to execute and subsequently deleted. Further research may show that a more feasible approach may be to queue the transaction until the mobile site is able to connect to its parent site, obtain authorisation for the transaction and then allow the transaction to execute.

4.3.   UPDATING AN MSPO

There are several problems in allowing an MSPO to be updated whilst disconnected from the federated database. We are concerned with the problem of integrity. Since an MSPO is not connected to the federated database, how can we be certain that an MSPO which has been updated whilst disconnected from the federated database has undergone a series of authorised modifications? One could argue that we can be sure the MSPO has maintained its integrity since it will only be used via the TCC.

Within the framework we have proposed so far, this is indeed the case, but usage of an MSPO limited. There will be properties of an MSPO which require authorisation in order to be modified. Since the MSPO is on a mobile site, connecting to the federated database to obtain authorisation may not always be feasible. Does this mean that one is denied the ability to update an MSPO property which requires authorisation, unless the mobile site can establish contact with the federated database? This is indeed the case if we are to be certain that integrity will be maintained.

An alternative to this approach may be to make use of a slightly modified TCC on the mobile site, modifications can be made to the way a TCC handles transactions in general. The TCC could allow transactions which require authorisation to simply be executed, whilst maintaining a log of all the activities of each transaction. Upon re-entry into the federated database the transaction log for the MSPO would be analysed and executed on the duplicate copy made of the MSPO before becoming mobile. If unauthorised modifications are identified, these transactions can simply be ignored. The duplicate copy of the MSPO, having undergone all the authorised transactions of the transaction log would then be permitted to re-enter the federated database. Figure 3 illustrates the proposed alternative to handling unauthorised transactions.

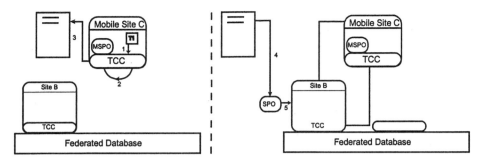

1. Request to execute transaction 'T1'.
2. Authorisation to execute the transaction is automatically granted.
3. The TCC logs the transaction.
4. Upon reconnection, the logged transactions are executed on the duplicate SPO. All unauthorised transactions are ignored.
5. If this task is completed successfully, the SPO is granted access into the federated database.

Figure 3   An alternative to handling unauthorised transactions.

4.4.   RE-ENTRY INTO THE FEDERATED DATABASE

Before an MSPO can be allowed back into the federated database, one has to be certain it is an MSPO which has undergone a series of authorised transactions and has, essentially, maintained its integrity.

Assuming the time that the mobile site has been disconnected has not exceeded the maximum time that it is allowed to be disconnected, each MSPO that is hosted by the mobile site will in turn undergo a re-entry process which will determine whether or not the MSPO will be allowed to re-enter the federated database.

The primary goal of the re-entry process is to ensure that the MSPO being re-introduced into the database has not had its integrity compromised and at the very least, is the MSPO that it claims to be. As the mobile site reconnects to its parent site, the MSPO will be moved from the mobile site to its originating site. The Unique Identifier (UI) of the SPO will then be extracted and a hash made of the object as well as hashes made of each of the values that require authorisation in order to me modified. The UI and the hashes will then be compared to the duplicated UI and hashes stored at the SPO's originating site before the SPO became mobile or after any authorised modifications made whilst the MSPO was mobile. If they are alike, the SPO will then undergo the second and final phase of the re-entry process.

Should the SPO fail the first phase of the re-entry process, the SPO will be denied re-entry into the database. Having failed the first phase, one can with certainty deduce that the integrity of the SPO has indeed been compromised. The SPO will be deleted and the duplicate copy made at its originating site will be used to re-introduce the SPO into the federated database, in its last uncompromised state.

The second phase of re-entry has the SPO undergo an order of operations which will ensure that any valid changes made to the SPO whilst mobile will now be saved and the SPO will be declared as being in a valid, uncompromised state. The new duplicate copy and hashes will simply replace the previous duplicate copy and hashes stored on the SPO's originating site.

5.   CONCLUSION

In this paper we have introduced the concept of Mobile Self Protecting Objects and have proposed an architecture within which it can be implemented. We have discussed how MSPOs can be used on mobile sites and how transactions requiring authorisation can be handled with the ultimate goal of ensuring that the integrity of the MSPO will always be maintained.

We have assumed throughout this paper that mobile sites will implement and trust the TCC. In doing so, we can be certain that the integrity of an MSPO will be maintained regardless of malicious intent or error.

References

[BAD95] B. R. Badrinath, Shirish Hemant Phatak, An Architecture for Mobile Databases,Rutgers University, Department of Computer Science, Technical report #DCS-TR-351 1995

[CFM95] Silvana Castano, Mariagrazia Fugini, Giancarlo Martella, Pierangela Samarati, Database Security, Addison-Wesley & ACM Press 1995

[CP85] Stefano Ceri and Guiseppe Pelagatti, Distributed databases - principles and systems, McGraw-Hill 1985

[OLI96] Martin S Olivier, Self-Protecting Objects in a Secure Federated Database, In Spooner, SA Demurjian and JE Dobson (eds), Database Security IX: Status and Prospects, 27-42, Chapman & Hall, 1996

[OLI97] Martin S Olivier, Secure Mobile Nodes in Federated Databasesbase, South African Computer Journal, 20, 11-17, 1997

[SL90] Amit P. Sheth, James A. Larson ACM Computing Surveys,Federated Database Systems for Managing Distributed, Heterogeneous, and Autonomous Databases, Vol. 22, No. 3, September 1990

[TIP00] Kimberly Tipton, Fortune 1000 Executives Forecast Dramatic Increase in Need for Mobile Communications, AVT Corporation News Release, http://www.mobiledelivery.com/pr_report.htm 2000

BUILDING ON SOLID FOUNDATIONS
An Information Security Case Study

EDO ROOS LINDGREEN*

University of Amsterdam
Department of Accountancy and Information Management
Roetersstraat 11, 1018 WB Amsterdam
Tel. +31-20-6567429, fax +31-20-6568800, e-mail roos.edo@kpmg.nl

* *Written in close co-operation with J.Acohen, A.J. de Boer, G. uit de Bosch and C. van Rinsum*

Key words: *Keywords: information security, BS 7799, corporate information security, integrated approach*

Abstract: *The paper gives a factual account of a two-year information security project based on the well-known BS 7799 carried out in The Netherlands. It describes the project organisation, the various sub-projects and the results achieved, and focuses on experiences from which other security professionals may potentially benefit.*

1.   INTRODUCTION

Spring 1998. Eight thirty in the morning. The financial director of a large company in the middle of the Netherlands runs into a traffic jam where there usually isn't one. In the distance, just about where the head office is located, he sees billowing black smoke and flashing lights. Just for a split second, the thought enters his mind: it couldn't be...

Soon it is clear that it's not a terrible fire at head office that's causing this commotion, but rather a huge tanker that has overturned on the A28 motorway. The driver has been taken away in a state of shock. The director starts his day with his first meeting, a little later than planned. Business as usual. But the uneasy feeling remains. What if it had been head office?

Papers on information security often start with a passage about the increasing importance of information technology in our society and the growing dependence that has resulted from this. This is normally followed by a description of the opportunities and risks of these new technological developments, and how these risks must be controlled in a responsible manner... You get the idea. We do live in interesting times. Never before has technology brought forth so many improvements in price and performance so consistently and for so long. Never before has a new technology penetrated to the heart of our society so swiftly and silently. And never before have we enjoyed the fruits of so much of these economic and social developments. These examples from daily life speak for themselves.

All these developments, however, have far-reaching effects for the field of information security[1]. On the one hand, we are dealing with the growing integration of smaller, faster and cheaper components, which results in environments that are increasingly difficult to protect. On the other hand, new technology is providing us with means to protect the fourth production factor better than ever, and by which we can learn more quickly from our experiences. In short: the game is becoming more difficult, but the players are getting better, and their techniques more powerful. And what is a better way to master the game than learning from the experiences of others?

Which brings us to the purpose of this paper: a description of a two-year project carried out by Dutch companies Bouwfonds and Stater in order to improve the security of their information and information systems. The structure of this paper is as follows. We will first look at the most important characteristics of Bouwfonds and Stater. This will be followed by a description of the approach used and a report on the Security & Continuity project which was carried out during the period 1998-2000. In this context, we will examine the project organisation, the various sub-projects and the results achieved. The next section, "Lessons learned", describes our positive experiences, from which others can potentially benefit. The final section includes a number of conclusions.

---

[1] In this article, information security is defined as the development, implementation and maintenance of a system of measures to protect the quality of information against specific threats. The notion of quality includes the aspects of confidentiality, integrity and availability.

2.   BOUWFONDS AND STATER

In the Netherlands, Bouwfonds is one of the major players in the field of real estate development, financing and management. To an increasing degree, the company's activities take place outside the Netherlands. Bouwfonds is organised into different business units, which focus on the company's specific core markets.

Bouwfonds' activities take place on both the personal and business markets. Personal market activities include the development and sale of residences, the granting of home mortgage loans and the management of residences for third parties. Bouwfonds' activities on the business market encompass the development, financing and management of offices and shopping centres. Bouwfonds has approximately 1,200 employees, a turnover of NLG 3.8 billion and a balance sheet total of more than NLG 29 billion. On the Dutch private capital market, the company attracts more than NLG 4 billion a year.

In the Netherlands, Bouwfonds is the largest risk-bearing developer of privately-owned homes. Its market share in the relevant sector (residences for purchase and expensive rentals) amounts to approximately 10%. Integral area development and cooperation with other market parties are increasing.

For owner-occupiers and investors, Bouwfonds develops office buildings, shopping centres and business premises. These activities include the development of new real estate, in addition to the redevelopment of existing real estate.

Bouwfonds ranks fifth in the Dutch market for home mortgage loans with a market share of around 5%. The company offers many types of mortgage loans, including both its own and those from third parties. The company also has partnership arrangements with insurers, where Bouwfonds provides the mortgage loan and the partner provides the insurance. Real estate and financing knowledge is also used in the provision of services to funds such as the Dutch National Restoration Fund and the Dutch National Green Fund.

In recent years, large investments were made in adopting state-of-the-art information technology in credit assessment and portfolio management. This allowed Bouwfonds to build up its competencies to become the first company in the Netherlands to launch portfolio management on the market as a separate service.

In 1997, Stater was established for this purpose: as an independent provider in the mortgage market. Since then, Stater has grown into an international company with more than 300 employees. It has its main office is in Amersfoort, the Netherlands, and a branch office in Bonn, Germany. The Stater Mortgage System (Stater Hypotheek Systeem – SHS) manages more than one million mortgage loans and is the market leader in this area.

Bouwfonds' activities have been accommodated in separate companies and clustered in three sub-holding companies. These sub-holding companies do not form a separate management level, and are headed by management that reports directly to the Executive Board. These companies are wholly-owned subsidiaries, with the exception of Bouwfonds Vastgoedmanagement and Hopman. Group-wide IT activities are accommodated in the BITS department (Bouwfonds IT Services). Within Bouwfonds, an important role will be played in IT by the Information Policy Platform, a group-wide consultative body for IT issues, in which the directors of the major operating companies are represented.

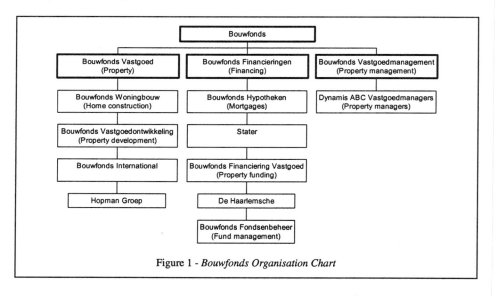

Figure 1 - *Bouwfonds Organisation Chart*

3.   FROM ANALYSIS TO SECURITY PLAN

The security project began in the summer of 1998, when Bouwfonds invited three consultancy groups to explain their approach and submit a proposal. After assessing the proposals, the company decided to implement a project based on KPMG's Corporate Information Security programme. This simple 'best practice' approach consists of eight consecutive stages.

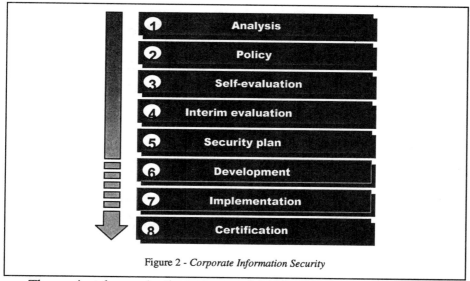

Figure 2 - *Corporate Information Security*

The project began in the autumn of 1998 with the implementation of stages 1 to 5. The objective was to perform an analysis, draw up a security policy, carry out a self-assessment and prepare a security plan.

A project group reporting directly to the Information Policy Platform was formed for this purpose. The project group consists of information managers from a number of leading operating companies, representatives of the IT organisation, the security manager and an external adviser.

A proposal was made to use the well-known Code of Practice for Information Security Management (British Standard 7799) as the basis for the security project. In The Netherlands, this standard has developed into the most widely accepted *de facto* standard for the control of information security within organisations. The BS 7799 covers the following aspects:
1. Policy
2. Organisation
3. Classification and management
4. Personnel
5. Physical security
6. Computer and network management
7. Access security for systems
8. Development and maintenance of systems
9. Continuity planning
10. Supervision

The purpose of the BS 7799 is to raise the level of security within organisations to a necessary minimum level and thus to promote mutual confidence between organisations and/or organisational units. In general terms, the BS 7799 is widely regarded as the most suitable basis for the certification of information security within organisations.

After a brief analysis of the business processes and information systems, the project group unanimously adopted the Dutch version of BS 7799. However, a prerequisite was that the standard would have to be customised, entailing additional measures being taken for specific applications, including the treasury application (these measures had, in fact, already been taken). The project group met once a fortnight and drafted a new information security policy, based on the BS 7799. The policy was officially approved by the Information Policy Platform in the autumn of 1998, after which it was formally approved by the Executive Board.

The project group then assessed the level of the security measure system within each operating company of Bouwfonds by means of a self-assessment questionnaire. The results of the self-assessment were discussed and used as basis for drawing up a security plan. This plan defined a number of sub-projects with clear aims, giving an outline of the resources required for the implementation of these sub-projects, stating the applicable prerequisites and the expected turnaround times. The plan was submitted to the Information Policy Platform and formally approved by the Bouwfonds management in the spring of 1999.

4.   DEVELOPMENT AND IMPLEMENTATION

A separate project was set up for the implementation of the security plan, corresponding with phases 6 and 7 in the Corporate Information Security programme. The project was known as Security & Continuity. In accordance with the project plan, the project included five identifiable sub-projects. Please refer to the table below.

Table 1 – Sub-projects

Sub-project	Objective
Continuity	Setting up operational continuity facilities for the Bouwfonds and Stater information systems.
IT security	Implementing proper security measures for the Bouwfonds and Stater computer networks and management systems.
Physical security	Proper physical security for the Bouwfonds and Stater buildings and premises.
Organisation and procedures	Designing, testing, accepting and implementing *procedures and guidelines* for a number of sub-areas.
Communication	Implementing a focused *communication programme* in the context of awareness and information with respect to the implementation of procedures and guidelines.

During 2000, a sixth sub-project was added:

Sub-project	Objective
Certification	Certification against BS 7799 of the different Bouwfonds and Stater operating companies.

4.1 Project organisation

The five sub-projects were to be carried out relatively independently of each other. The project organisation was solid, but simple: experienced and independently operating sub-project leaders reporting to a general project manager who was responsible to the Steering Committee. The choice was for a pragmatic form of project management, with a minimum of superfluous paperwork in the form of detailed schedules and extensive reporting. Important decisions were submitted for approval to the Information Policy Platform in advance.

In addition, two expert teams were set up during the implementation phase in order to monitor the quality of the delivered products and, at the same time, create maximum support within the operating companies. These expertise teams comprised specialist representatives from a number of leading operating companies. The *business expertise team* focused on management aspects; it was therefore no coincidence that the composition of this team showed similarities to that of the project group for phases 1-5. The *IT expertise team* focused on IT-specific matters. This also involved regular meetings to discuss specific technical details that were less relevant for the general management.

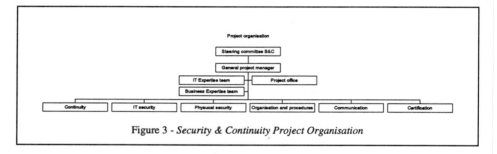

Figure 3 - *Security & Continuity Project Organisation*

5.   RESULTS

Briefly, it can be stated that all the project objectives have been achieved, whereby some of the turnaround times in the original plan were exceeded. Below, the results of the individual sub-projects are reported, including the way in which the results were achieved. Particular attention is focused on the Continuity sub-project, which, in all aspects, had the greatest impact and required the biggest effort.

5.1   Continuity sub-project

The sub-project Continuity started with making an inventory of the demands on the continuity of the Bouwfonds and Stater information systems. Two important principles were formulated in this context, both of which were approved by the Information Policy Platform:

A. A maximum permitted downtime of 24 hours should apply to the most important systems.

B. Data older than one hour should not be lost.

The maximum permitted downtime is defined as: the time that lapses from the moment a calamity occurs until the system is fully operational again.

These stringent requirements, resulting from the fact that Bouwfonds and Stater are responsible for critical production data of third parties, had far-reaching effects on the preferred solution. A brief analysis showed that the traditional contingency approach fell short of the demands. This approach involves making daily backups, which are then stored at an external contingency location. In the event of a calamity, the backups at the contingency location are retrieved, whereby production can be resumed at the contingency location. Since the retrieval of the backups, given the volume of data at the time, would take more than 24 hours, it meant that requirement A could not be satisfied. And because the backups could only be made once a day, the requirement B could also not be satisfied. Mirroring was the only option left. This involves the production details being stored in real-time at a secondary external location. In the event of a calamity, no retrieval of backups would be required, which means that production could be resumed immediately.

This basic decision to implement a mirroring solution resulted in a technical challenge. As is often the case nowadays, the critical production details and information systems of Bouwfonds and Stater are spread over dozens of servers with divergent characteristics, from Windows NT on Intel machines to Unix and OpenVMS on the Digital Alpha platform.

Achieving a mirroring solution in the heterogeneous environment did not appear possible without an extensive change to the IT infrastructure. This change involved concentrating the storage of data on a limited number of storage systems with a high capacity, high performance and a high level of reliability.

A number of suppliers were invited to submit a proposal, and after a formal selection procedure on the basis of objective criteria, the EMC proposal was chosen. This solution consisted of two Symmetrix 3830 storage systems, two Symmetrix 3930 storage systems and two Connectrix switches. The latter was required to connect the great number of different servers in BITS and Stater to the storage systems. EMC technology is used by many large organisations to store critical data. The order involved many millions of guilders. The total storage capacity was around 22.6 Terabyte.

The remainder of this sub-project was then scheduled in three phases. During phase 1, the primary storage systems were installed, and data migrated from the old discs to the EMC environment. During phase 2, the secondary storage systems were installed and the primary and secondary systems connected to each other by means of a high-speed data communication link. During phase 3, the required redundant processor capacity was acquired and the continuity plans developed.

In the autumn of 1999, EMC installed the primary storage systems with the support of IT specialists from Bouwfonds and Stater. The servers were fitted with special interface cards, enabling connection to the Symmetrix and Connectrix equipment. A number of technical problems manifested themselves during the process, which were resolved in close cooperation with the supplier. Flexibility and the ability to improvise proved to be great assets.

Some of the problems and their solutions appear to be par for the course for projects like this. Some of the older servers, for instance, were not supported by EMC, resulting in new servers having to be acquired, for which the costs were shared. Several other problems were compatibility-related and were eventually solved as new driver software became available. A number problems were more mundane. For instance, the power supply in the Stater building initially appeared insufficient for supplying all the equipment with electricity. While waiting for the electricity company to upgrade the electricity supply, a diesel generator, reserved for the millennium change, was used and the kitchen equipment of the staff canteen connected to it. This released enough capacity for the EMC equipment.

There were no significant problems with the installation of the primary storage systems. The same applied to the production data migration, including the software files. Some delays were caused by the so-called frozen period prior to the millennium change, a period during which no modifications were allowed to the systems any more. This resulted in a great deal of necessary maintenance and control work having to be carried out during October and November, which meant that the available staff capacity came under a lot of pressure.

In December, the migration took place and phase 1 was completed. At the eleventh hour of the financial year, it was decided to expand the storage capacity, at reasonable terms. The millennium change went without a hitch for Bouwfonds.

Phase 2 started with an investigation into the most appropriate contingency location for Bouwfonds and Stater, as well as the most suitable data communication links between these locations. The choice for a location was complicated by the simultaneous development of plans to relocate parts of Bouwfonds and Stater. Finally, a situation was chosen whereby Bouwfonds in Hoevelaken and Stater in Amersfoort would function as each other's contingency location. A costing exercise was done for the data communication link over a distance of six kilometres. This revealed that laying an own fibre optics link woud be many times cheaper than renting the required capacity from a large supplier, if they can deliver at all; the annual depreciation on an investment of a couple of hundred thousand guilders is considerably lower than the annual rental charges. A specialised company was commissioned to acquire the necessary permit, do the necessary digging, lay the cable and complete the installation. The link was up and running four months later.

In July 2000, the required modifications to the computing centres in Hoevelaken and Amersfoort were also completed. The secondary EMC systems were installed and connected to the fibre optics link. This was followed by automatic synchronisation between the primary and secondary Symmetrix systems. In the summer of 2000, the link was operational. Real-time mirroring was a fact. The original objective was not achieved in one respect: the data loss in the event of a calamity was not limited to one hour, but to zero hours.

The required redundant processor capacity will be acquired during phase 3. The necessary continuity plans will also be drawn up. Phase 3 will be completed early in 2001.

5.2   IT Security sub-project

The IT security sub-project commenced with a quick scan, carried out by KPMG. The quick scan revealed the most important vulnerabilities in the IT infrastructure, in which the focus was on management systems and networks. These vulnerabilities were analysed and systematically rectified during the following months. This included the configuration of active network components, the removal of specific access possibilities and the installation of special software for the safe exchange of files.

Part of this sub-project involved researching new authentication techniques, including token (hardware) solutions and digital certificates. The most important conclusion from this research was that digital certificates are gaining ground, but that the market for new authentication techniques is still too fluid to standardise at this point in time.

5.3   Physical Security sub-project

As part of this sub-project, the various Bouwfonds and Stater offices were visited, which revealed shortcomings in the physical security. A plan to rectify these shortcomings was drawn up in conjunction with the responsible building manager. These plans were implemented during the subsequent months.

5.4   Organisation and Procedures sub-project

As part of this sub-project, KPMG drew up procedures and guidelines in the field of information security, which will be published in a Information Security Manual. The procedures and guidelines are partly a formalisation of existing practice. Parts of the Manual were continuously reviewed and commented upon by the business expertise team in order to guarantee coordination with the operating companies.

The Information Security Manual was completed in December 2000. The Board of Directors formally approved the Manual in early-2001 and handed it over to the group security manager. The security manager is responsible for distribution on paper, CD-ROM and via the company intranet, Insite.

Actual implementation of the Manual remains the responsibility of the individual operating companies. For this purpose, a local information security manager was appointed and trained for each operating company.

5.5   Communication sub-project

As part of this sub-project, a communications plan was developed in order to introduce a few basic rules and to increase general security awareness. The Information Policy Platform judged an initial version of the plan as too creative. A second, more sober version was approved and implemented after formal approval of the Information Security Manual.

Each Bouwfonds member of staff received a booklet containing guidelines and handy tips, with a covering letter from the Executive Board, in April. The booklet reflects the house style of Bouwfonds and has the Bouwfonds art collection as theme. In the months thereafter, BITS installed screensavers with password security on the PC of each Bouwfonds member of staff.

5.6   Certification sub-project

A separate plan of action was drawn up for the Certification sub-project as well, based in part on the applicable certification schema. As part of this sub-project, the external accountant, Ernst & Young, performed a pre-certification audit in July and August 2000. The audit was based on self-assessments carried out by the local information security managers. The audit resulted in a substantial list of improvement actions, which were carefully scrutinised, identifying each improvement action as (a) already realised, (b) a quick win, (c) a slow gain, or (d) an accepted non-conformity. Quick wins and slow gains were planned and realised in the months that followed.

KPMG Certification then performed the certification process. This process consists of two major activities. First, the certifying organisation conducts a documentation audit to establish whether the organisation's own requirements comply with BS 7799. Second, the certifying organisation conducts an implementation audit to verify whether the organisation to be certified complies with its own requirements. During the implementation audit, much attention is paid to the quality of the underlying management processes, the quality of which must be demonstrated by written evidence (minutes, reports, organisation charts and so forth). Lastly, the organisation to be certified issues a statement of compliance in which the Executive Board formally declares to comply with the BS 7799. The certification process resulted in a number of critical and non-critical non-conformities, many of which were related to the quality of the management process. Bouwfonds' information security managers addressed the non-conformities with vigour. In the spring of 2001, the certification process was completed and Bouwfonds was successfully filed for certification. The certificate was issued on May 16 by Mr. P.L. Overbeek acting on behalf of KPMG Certification and was received by mr. J.J.M. Reijrink of the Executive Board during a brief but joyous ceremony. The certificate has a lifetime of three years. The certifying organisation promised to return after six months to re-establish the validity of the certificate.

6.   LESSONS LEARNED

As with all major projects, an evaluation was carried out during the last phase of this project. The most important conclusion was that the chosen plan of action had led to the desired results. All objectives were achieved.

As stated before, a quick and pragmatic approach was chosen for the planning and management of the different sub-projects. This approach made it possible to respond quickly to changing circumstances during the run of the project. For instance, the project was affected by the ongoing developments, unforeseen technical challenges, preparations for the millennium transition and, last but not least, the takeover of Bouwfonds by ABN-AMRO in the autumn of 1999. (In addition, the Security & Continuity project was also reviewed during the accompanying due diligence investigation, which provided a valuable second opinion for the client and project organisation and resulted in a positive outcome.)

The most important choices made during the project proved to be the right ones in retrospect. Certification proved very useful in the sense that it has given this project a very clear and tangible goal, stimulating all parties to keep the project running to completion. It seemed the right choice to group the project objectives into separate, clearly defined sub-projects. This modular approach made it possible to carry out the different activities relatively independently from each other, and limited communication between the different projects to the bare essential. All parties involved positively evaluated the commitment shown by senior management, the efforts of the staff involved in the project, the quality of the project managers and the co-operation between the different organisational units and the external parties. Priorities in this respect were maintaining the quality in the relationship with the suppliers, as well as dealing with the heterogeneous interests of the different operating companies. During the project, several delays were observed. In virtually all cases, these delays were caused by the emergence of business activities with a higher priority, which is not unusual in a security project.

Over and above the fact that the objectives were achieved, the project also had a number of other side effects. The most important bonuses are:

- Reliability – by employing the mirroring solution, no data at all is lost in the event of a calamity.

- Standardisation – the IT infrastructure has been standardised and updated.

- Centralisation – during the course of the project, a number of locally managed servers were brought under central management to the full satisfaction of the operating companies.

- Performance – installation of the EMC equipment resulted in a measurable improvement in the performance of certain applications; there has been a 30 – 50% improvement in batch processing.

- Flexibility – it now proves easier to cope with an increase demand in storage space as a result of the new storage infrastructure.

- Efficiency – the new storage infrastructure leads to a more efficient use of the storage capacity and reduced maintenance costs.

All of this does not mean that the project ran without any hitch whatsoever. As with any project, this one also showed evidence of the usual technical problems, political considerations, changes of management and human factors– issues that can never be properly covered in a paper like this, yet which make the implementation of a project such as this one so fascinating.

7.   CONCLUSIONS

A structured and consistent approach, fully backed by senior management, has led to encouraging results. Security has been brought up to standard at all levels. In addition, an organic contingency solution was achieved using mirroring, which is based on very advanced storage technology. This guarantees the continuity of a critical, heterogeneous IT environment.

This project again showed that information security is no longer a freestanding speciality, but that it is part and parcel of the day-to-day management of a company. An integral security project such as this one carries the risk that security is seen as an isolated problem. In the case of Bouwfonds, however, the chosen approach has resulted in the problem now being recognised and tackled at almost all levels of the organisation. The BS 7799 turned out to be a very solid foundation for projects like this. In addition, continuous top management commitment and a high degree of user involvement were identified as critical success factors.

Also, in this context, the human factor remains one of the biggest priorities. As technology becomes more complex and the arsenal of tools becomes more powerful, the dependence on the knowledge, discipline and precision of the users and system controllers will increase. Implementing a centrally led communication programme is no longer sufficient. The necessary attention and a positive attitude from management are at least equally important. The same applies to performing systematic monitoring of compliance with the policy.

8. ACKNOWLEDGEMENTS

This project would not have been possible without the efforts and commitment of a great number of people. Special mention is due to, among others, the following people, in alphabetical order: R. van Aart, G. Bos, J.H. Deesker, R. Douwes, J. Gerkema, T. Heusdens, P. Hoffman, H. Kleinhoven, L. van der Meché, F. van Meijgaarden, P. Lissenburg, G. Peters-Meijer, M. Pouw, F. Schuit, A. Spruitenburg, J.P. de Smeth, J. Veenstra, the staff of EMC, KPMG, Ernst & Young and Van der Donk who were involved in this project, and the driver of the tanker on the A28.

USING GYPSIE, GYNGER AND VISUAL GNY TO ANALYZE CRYPTOGRAPHIC PROTOCOLS IN SPEAR II

Elton Saul
Data Network Architectures Laboratory
University of Cape Town, South Africa
esaul@cs.uct.ac.za

Andrew Hutchison
Data Network Architectures Laboratory
University of Cape Town, South Africa
hutch@cs.uct.ac.za

Abstract   The development of cryptographic logics to analyze security protocols has provided one technique for ensuring the correctness of these protocols. However, it is commonly acknowledged that analysis using a modal logic such as GNY tends to be inaccessible and obscure for the uninitiated. In this paper we describe the SPEAR II graphically-based security protocol engineering environment that can be used to easily conduct GNY analyses. SPEAR II consists of three primary components: a protocol specification environment (GYPSIE), a GNY statement construction interface (Visual GNY) and a Prolog-based GNY analysis engine (GYNGER). In contrast to other tools, SPEAR II offers a multi-dimensional approach to protocol engineering, integrating protocol design and analysis into one consistent and unified interface. The interface and techniques used within this tool are built on the foundation of previous experience with the original SPEAR tool and GNY analysis research. We also show how the SPEAR II tool is used to conduct a GNY analysis and how it distances protocol engineers from any associated syntactical issues, allowing them to focus more on the associated semantics and distil the critical issues that arise. By freeing individuals to focus on an analysis, instead of hampering them with the necessary syntax, we can ensure that the fundamental concepts and advantages related to GNY analysis are kept in mind and applied as well.

Keywords: Security Protocol Modelling, Protocol Engineering, GNY Logic

1.   INTRODUCTION

Analysis methods for cryptographic protocols have predominantly focused on detecting information leakage, rather than determining whether a protocol attains its stated goals. However, security protocols often fall short of achieving their intended objectives, usually for very subtle reasons [2]. As a result of this fact, cryptographic logics have been developed to aid in determining whether protocols actually fulfil their intended goals [5].

The inherent appeal in using modal logics stems from their simplicity and effectiveness for analyzing cryptographic protocols. Logics can be systematically applied to reason about the working of protocols, often helping to reveal missing assumptions, deficiencies or redundancies. This can then lead to the protocol, the assumptions or the original goals being re-evaluated, after which the inference rules can be reapplied to determine whether the goals are attainable after these modifications have been made.

The BAN modal logic [1] popularized the notion of using logics to detect flaws and redundancies in protocols. It has been labelled as a success by many commentators [6, 11, 4] and has been used to find flaws in several protocols. BAN spawned the creation of a number of related logics, each of which has tried to improve on or add to its underlying premises. A popular descendant of BAN is GNY [7, 8].

However, due to the complexity of the GNY syntax, notation and inference rules, it is commonly acknowledged that analysis with GNY tends to be inaccessible and obscure for the uninitiated. Often it requires experience and insight to determine what the desirable and appropriate initial and final conditions for a given protocol should be. Also, the actual analysis phase during which inference rules are applied can be very tedious and error prone when carried out by hand. Thus, the opportunity exists to create tools that will support analysis efforts by guiding the process from an appropriate starting state to the required final state. Such a system would help to make the rigorous analysis of security protocols more accessible and thus contribute to the overall security level of cryptographic protocols that currently exist and are being designed.

In this paper we will describe the SPEAR II cryptographic protocol analysis tool which we have developed. SPEAR II allows an individual to easily conduct a GNY-based protocol analysis using an intuitive visual interface. This interface offers a multi-dimensional approach to cryptographic protocol analysis, unifying the design and analysis phases of protocol engineering into one consistent and easy-to-use system. We will elaborate on the core components of SPEAR II and show how they help to distance protocol engineers from the syntactical element of GNY analysis, allowing them to focus more on the associated semantics and distil the critical issues which arise.

The remainder of this paper is organized as follows. In Section 2 we give a brief introduction to GNY analysis. Section 3 gives an overview of some tools that can be used for logic-based analysis. In Section 4 we will describe all of the current SPEAR II components, and then show how the SPEAR II environment is used in an analysis in Section 5. We conclude in Section 7.

2.   PRINCIPLES OF GNY ANALYSIS

An analysis with GNY is very similar to one carried out with BAN. However, one significant improvement of GNY over BAN is that it defines an abstract 'protocol parser' which helps to derive a form of the protocol more suitable for manipulation. The major steps carried out before analyzing a security protocol with GNY are enumerated below:

1. Any implicit information conveyed by a protocol formula is represented logically by the attachment of an extension to the formula.

2. A star is placed in front of all formulae containing secrets that the receiving principal is *not* the first to convey in the current session of the protocol. The star also indicates that it is the first time that the receiving principal receives the formula in the current session.

3. The initial belief and possession sets of each principal are constructed. The possession set consists of all formulae available to the principal, while the belief set includes the current beliefs of the principal.

4. The desired final possession and belief sets for each principal are specified based on the design goals of the protocol.

Once these steps have been performed, an analysis can proceed. Each analysis essentially consists of deriving a series of assertions, each assertion being obtained by the application of the GNY inference rules to the assertions already contained within the belief and possession sets of a principal. After each assertion is derived, it is added to either the belief or possession set of the relevant principal. Once the analysis is complete the belief and possession sets will contain the final state of each principal after the protocol has run to completion. This information can then be compared to the desired final conditions to determine whether the protocol has achieved its intended goals.

3.   LOGIC-BASED ANALYSIS TOOLS

A number of tools exist to carry out automated logic-based analyses. However, the interface to these tools is often textual, and in cases where a GUI is used to define the protocol to be analyzed, the GNY logic statements are still defined using textual commands.

Convince is an automated toolset that facilitates the modelling and analysis of cryptographic protocols [9]. A protocol is specified by using an integrated commercial GUI system, however GNY statements which are used for analysis must still be defined through textual annotations.

A Prolog-based analysis tool was created to facilitate in a GNY analysis [12]. However, this tool again makes use of textual input schemes which are then analyzed by the Prolog program.

The SPEAR multi-dimensional protocol analysis tool allows a user to specify a protocol in an intuitive graphical environment [3]. Logic-based analysis is conducted using BAN. However, even though the tool has a GUI for defining the protocol, BAN statements have to be constructed in a textual form. Primitive assistance is provided when constructing BAN statements by providing the user with a list of operators and operands which can be added to the current BAN statement.

4.   THE SPEAR II FRAMEWORK

The SPEAR II framework aims to provide a unified graphically-based environment within which security protocols can be specified, analyzed and then implemented. A major aim of the framework is to ensure speed and ease of use, but at the same time ensure that quality protocol engineering takes place. At present, the framework consists of three primary components, each of which will be described in the sections that follow.

4.1.   GYPSIE

GYPSIE is a graphically-based cryptographic protocol specification environment [13]. Using GYPSIE, a designer can specify a security protocol by employing three basic components. All of these components are rendered on a design canvas in a style reminiscent of SDL and MSCs. The graphical representation of each of these components has been selected to provide the most intuitive and simplistic representation of the real-world analogues. These canvas components are listed below:

- *Principals*, which send and receive messages.

- *Messages*, which contain formulae such as nonces and hashes.

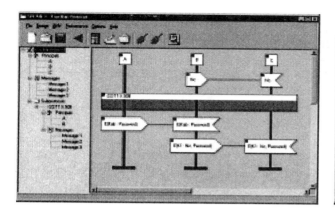 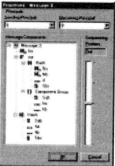

Figure 1   An illustration of the high-level protocol view on the left and the component view on the right.

- *Subprotocols*, which contain further principals and messages.

The high-level protocol view (illustrated in Figure 1) allows a designer to manipulate principals, messages and subprotocols that are found in the protocol model. Messages, principals and subprotocols can be dragged and dropped on the canvas and imported from other protocols which are included in the subprotocol hierarchy. Messages and subprotocols are ordered in time, based on when they are sent, received or called. All design operations can be carried out through the use of pull-down or pop-up menus, depending on the user's preference. The high-level view also has full undo and redo capabilities, and allows a protocol model to be saved, loaded or exported to a number of formats. It is also fully customizable and allows users to select the colours for each component, dragging styles and message display options.

The more detailed component view (shown in Figure 1) hierarchically displays the formulae within an individual message as a structured tree-view. Within this tree-view, formulae can be manipulated, edited, deleted, reordered and dragged and dropped onto encryption, function or grouping nodes. Thirteen primary formula types exist:

- *Non-terminal* formulae include functions, hashes, symmetric encryptions, public-key encryptions, private-key encryptions and groups.

- *Terminal* formulae include nonces, timestamps, shared secrets, symmetric keys, public keys, private keys and user-defined types.

Cut, copy and paste facilities exist within both the high-level and component views, allowing designers to copy or move formulae between messages and subprotocols. Within the component view, tooltips aid users by displaying the contents of non-terminal formulae when hovering over them. In the high-level view, tooltips are used to display message formulae when hovering over a message, as the message component on the canvas may be shortened to save screen real-estate.

A number of other useful features are included in GYPSIE. The 'component tracker' allows a designer to highlight all of the places where a given formula appears on the design canvas. A navigation bar on the left side of the high-level view aids users in visualizing the structure of a given protocol. GYPSIE also includes the ability to calculate synchronous and optimal rounds [10] for the specified protocol.

4.2.   GYNGER

GYNGER is a Prolog-based GNY analysis engine that uses forward-chaining techniques to derive all of the possible GNY statements applicable to a given protocol and set of initial assumptions. The analyzer is based on the one presented in [12], however, it implements more GNY inference rules (71 in total) and uses an improved syntax to facilitate the use of advanced GNY constructs.

To analyze a protocol with GYNGER, one must supply the protocol message steps and the initial belief and possession sets. Any target goals may also be specified. When the analyzer is invoked, the GNY inference rules are applied to the current set of GNY statements. When no more statements can be derived, the analysis process terminates. For those goals which were successful, a proof is generated listing all of the statements and inference rules used to derive the result. A list of all of the derived statements can also be generated.

4.3.   VISUAL GNY

The Visual GNY environment (illustrated in Figure 2) makes use of structured trees to represent GNY statements [14]. For each principal within a given protocol specification, up to four sets of structured trees are created, two for the storage of initial beliefs and possessions, and another two for the storage of target beliefs and possessions. A further four sets of trees can be used to store the successful beliefs, successful possessions, failed beliefs and failed possessions for each principal upon the completion of a successful GNY analysis. A set of structured trees is also created for every formula that has extensions, these extensions being defined in the Visual GNY environment.

Five tabbed panes are used to guide a user through the process of specifying initial GNY assumptions, goals and analyzing a protocol. Within

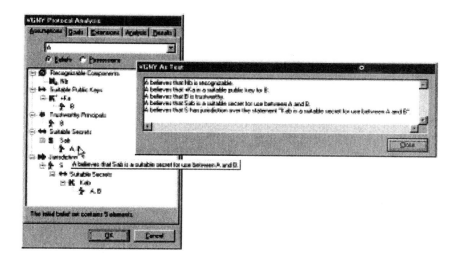

Figure 2   The Visual GNY environment.

each of these tabbed panes, a drop-down combo-box and a selection of radio buttons are used to select the appropriate set of structured trees to modify or view. The currently selected set of structured trees is displayed in a tree-view component centered within the client area of the tabbed pane. Changing either the combo-box or radio button selection changes the set of structured trees being displayed in the tree-view. A label situated below the tree-view indicates the number of GNY statements represented by the set of structured trees displayed in the tree view. All interaction with the structured tree takes place through pop-up menus that are dynamically constructed depending on the selected tree node.

The pop-up menus that are used in the Visual GNY environment are constructed dynamically so as to guide a user as she constructs the structured tree representation of a given GNY statement. Commands on a pop-up menu present a user with a choice of GNY statement types, principal names and message formulae to include in a structured tree. The structured trees are always ensured of being syntactically correct as the pop-up menus used in their construction reveal only the commands applicable to the currently selected node.

The Visual GNY environment attempts to structure and organize GNY analyses. The tabbed panes give an indication of the information required for an analysis, and are roughly laid out in the order that this information would be supplied. Nodes within a given structured tree can be expanded or collapsed as required. If a node contains children then

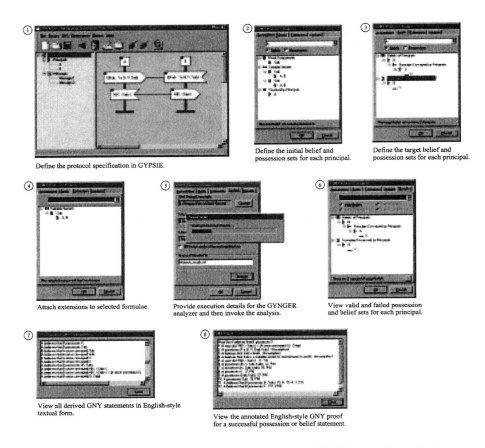

Figure 3   Steps undertaken when conducting a GNY protocol analysis.

a clickable token is displayed to its left. Clicking on this token allows
the node to be collapsed or expanded, thus allowing a user to control
the amount of information which is presented. In this way the level of
detail provided by the interface can be varied appropriately.

GNY statements created within the Visual GNY environment can
be exported to an English-style textual format, a mathematical-style
LaTeX format, or to GYNGER-compatible Prolog statements. When
hovering a mouse pointer over the tree node that terminates a given
GNY statement in a structured tree, a tooltip containing the English-
style text representing the statement is displayed. Besides this aid, a
user can also view all of the statements contained in a given tree-view
as English-style text in a pop-up window. This feature is activated from
the pop-up menus.

5.   GNY ANALYSIS WITH SPEAR II

In Figure 3 we sketch the steps that are undertaken during a typical analysis session. Such a session normally begins by specifying the principals, messages and formulae of the protocol in question within the GYPSIE specification environment. Once this phase has been completed, the Visual GNY environment is invoked and the initial assumptions and goals of each principal are specified as required. Extensions are also appended to formulae. Once all of the necessary preconditions have been defined, details such as the location of the Prolog interpreter, the location of the GNY rules Prolog source, working directories and output files are defined within the *Analysis* tabbed pane. Upon the initiation of the analysis process, the structured GNY trees are all translated into a GYNGER-compatible Prolog syntax, the GNY protocol parser is invoked, and the analyzer is then called with the relevant parameters. The Visual GNY environment monitors the analysis thread, and when it is complete, retrieves the results from the output files, parses these results, and then constructs the appropriate structured trees to display in the *Results* pane. Proofs and the list of all derived statements are also stored.

As we can see, a typical analysis session is very visual, with the graphical environment being used as much as possible to aid and guide the user. The *Results* tab is only displayed if an analysis has been conducted, and is hidden if any deletions are made from the GNY preconditions. To view the proof for a valid target goal, one merely needs to right-click on the terminal node of the statement's structured tree representation and then select the *View GNY Proof* menu item. To view all of the GNY statements derived during the most recent analysis, the button in the lower right of the *Analysis* tabbed pane is pressed. All of the constructed GNY statements and analysis results are saved together with the GYPSIE protocol specification. The analysis results are also saved to an output file defined within the *Analysis* tabbed pane. The undo and redo feature within GYPSIE is very useful for protocol analysis, since it allows a user to conduct analyses on variations of the same protocol. For instance, an analysis can be conducted with a certain formula contained within the protocol messages. This formula can then be deleted and another analysis conducted, with the two results being compared at the end. If the first results are better, then the deletion of the formula can be undone. In this way, we can determine whether a given formula is redundant with respect to its effect on helping to achieve the protocol goals.

6.   EXPERIENCES WITH USING SPEAR II

Over the past few months we have conducted a number of usability and practical usage experiments with SPEAR II. The usability experiments tested the interface of the Visual GNY environment and the ease with which individuals work within the GYPSIE modelling environment. Besides these user experiments, we have also tested the GYNGER analyzer and used it to analyze a wide variety of authentication protocols, as well as information exchange protocols. Some of these protocols include, the Needham Schroeder and Voting Protocols [8], the Wide Mouth Frog, Yahalom and Kerberos Protocols [1], as well as a number of authentication protocols from [10]. All the results from our analyses worked out as expected and returned accurate results and proofs.

The Visual GNY experiments returned some interesting results. We tested the interface on fifteen fourth-year Computer Science students who had taken a course in network security and protocol analysis with GNY. The last time any of these students had used GNY was almost six months prior to the experiment. They were each asked to specify a set of GNY statements in both conventional mathematical syntax and structured tree notation using the Visual GNY environment. On average, they specified 78% of the GNY statements correctly using mathematical notation, and 98% correctly using the Visual GNY environment. Only substitution errors were made when using the Visual GNY environment, as syntactic correctness correctness is enforced by the interface. When we asked these students to translate Visual GNY and mathematical style statements into English-style text, they got approximately 85% correct on average. This demonstrates that Visual GNY does not improve the readability of GNY statements. However, this is not much of an issue, as the tooltips and 'View GNY Statements as Text' features both display the constructed GNY structured trees as English-style text.

Experiments conducted with the GYPSIE interface set out to test how individuals interacted with the environment and how effectively they could specify protocols. We made use of another batch of twenty fourth-year Computer Science students who had all studied network security techniques. They were asked to specify three protocols: a voting protocol, an authentication protocol and the Needham-Schroeder protocol. On average, 0.5 mistakes were made in the voting protocol, 0.20 in the authentication protocol, and 0.65 in the Needham-Schroder protocol. The average construction times were 300 seconds, 378 seconds, and 589 seconds respectively. As evidenced by these figures, the GYPSIE environment facilitates accurate protocol construction, and intuitively we can assume that it will make individuals more productive and more effective than they would be in a text-based system, since they do not need to concern themselves with syntactical issues but can instead focus on the protocol at hand and its associated semantics.

7.   CONCLUSION

Security protocol engineers need to be familiar with security protocol analysis techniques and must also be able to effectively put these into practice. However, to be useful an analysis method must also be usable. We cannot expect individuals to be able to readily recall the syntax associated with a modal logic such as GNY or the plethora of inference rules used in an analysis, as this syntactical knowledge is often forgotten after it has not been applied for a while. Instead, the associated semantic issues and an understanding of how an analysis occurs should be the focus of an individual's analysis arsenal, tools and reference material being used to fill in any syntactical gaps.

There are a number of tools that can be used to carry out automated GNY protocol analysis [12, 9]. However, an impediment to using most of these is the construction of the specification which describes the protocol messages, formulae, initial assumptions and target goals. Supplying this information is not always a simple and straight-forward task and its prompt, efficient and error-free delivery often depends on the type of software being used. For this reason, the use of software that helps to distance protocol engineers from the syntactical element of protocol analysis, allowing them to focus more on the underlying critical issues, should be encouraged.

A formal analysis method should not just be studied and forgotten. Instead, the security community should be encouraged to develop tools that facilitate and encourage its use by a broad spectrum of individuals. When creating such tools, we should bear in mind that they should promote information recall, not require it. A tremendous amount of research has been carried out on security protocol analysis techniques [6], but how much of this research actually gets used in the field by the engineers who work there? Let's not allow good techniques to go unused. By encouraging more protocol analysis techniques to be applied, we will encourage the development of more robust and secure protocols.

Thus, by leveraging specially developed tools and techniques, a large portion of the difficulties that individuals encounter when using formal methods can be resolved. The SPEAR II tool [1] is a graphically-based analysis environment within which GNY protocol analysis can be conducted. SPEAR II places a user-friendly front-end on the GNY analysis process, thus freeing individuals to focus more on an analysis and the issues related thereto, instead of having them bogged down in syntax and tedious inference rule application. We hope to continue development of the SPEAR II framework by adding more analysis techniques and ensuring that these techniques can be used by protocol engineers when implementing and designing network security protocols.

Notes

1. Available from http://www.cs.uct.ac.za/Research/DNA/SPEAR2.

References

[1] M. Abadi, M. Burrows, and R. Needham. A Logic of Authentication. In *Proceedings of the Royal Society*, Series A, 426, 1871, pages 233 – 271, December 1989.

[2] M. Abadi and R. Needham. Prudent Engineering Practice for Cryptographic Protocols. *IEEE Transactions on Software Engineering*, 22(1):6 – 15, January 1996.

[3] J.P. Beckmann, P. De Goede, and A.C.M. Hutchison. SPEAR: Security Protocol Engineering and Analysis Resources. In *DIMACS Workshop on Design and Formal Verification of Security Protocols*. Rutgers University, September 1997.

[4] J. Clark and J. Jacob. *A Survey of Authentication Protocol Literature: Version 1.0*, November 1997.

[5] V.D. Gligor, L. Gong, R. Kailar, and S. Stubblebine. Logics for Cryptographic Protocols – Virtues and Limitations. In *Proceedings of the Fourth IEEE Computer Security Foundations Workshop*, pages 219 – 226, Franconia, New Hampshire, October 1991. IEEE Computer Society Press.

[6] P. Georgiadis, S. Gritzalis, and D. Spinellis. Security Protocols Over Open Networks and Distributed Systems: Formal Methods for Their Analysis, Design and Verification. *Computer Communications*, 22(8):695 – 707, May 1999.

[7] L. Gong, R. Needham, and R. Yahalom. Reasoning about Belief in Cryptographic Protocols. In *Proceedings of the 1990 IEEE Symposium on Research in Security and Privacy*, pages 234 – 248, Oakland, California, 1990. IEEE Computer Society Press.

[8] L. Gong. *Cryptographic Protocols for Distributed Systems*. PhD thesis, University of Cambridge, April 1990.

[9] R. Lichota, G. Hammonds, and S.H. Brackin. Verifying the Correctness of Cryptographic Protocols using Convince. In *Proceedings of*

the Twelfth IEEE Computer Security Applications Conference, pages 117 – 128. IEEE Computer Society Press, 1996.

[10] L. Gong Lower Bounds on Messages and Rounds for Network Authentication Protocols. In *Proceedings of the 1st ACM Conference on Computer and Communications Security*, pages 26 – 37, Fairfax, Virginia, November 1993.

[11] C.A. Meadows. Formal Verification of Cryptographic Protocols: A Survey. In *Advances in Cryptology - Asiacrypt '94*, pages 133 – 150. Springer-Verlag, 1995.

[12] A. Mathuria, R. Safavi-Naini, and P. Nickolas. On the Automation of GNY Logic. In *Proceedings of the 18th Australian Computer Science Conference*, volume 17, pages 370 – 379, Glenelg, South Australia, February 1995.

[13] E. Saul and A.C.M. Hutchison. A Generic Graphical Specification Environment for Security Protocol Modelling. In *Proceedings of the Sixth Annual Working Conference on Information Security*, pages 311 – 320, Beijing, China, August 2000. Kluwer Academic Publishers.

[14] E. Saul and A.C.M. Hutchison. A Graphical Environment for the Facilitation of Logic-Based Security Protocol Analysis. *South African Computer Journal*, (26):196 – 200, November 2000.

SECURITY VULNERABILITIES AND SYSTEM INTRUSIONS
The need for Automatic Response Frameworks

S.M.FURNELL, M.PAPADAKI, G.MAGKLARAS and A.ALAYED
Network Research Group,
Department of Communication and Electronic Engineering,
University of Plymouth,
Plymouth,
United Kingdom,
Tel: +44 1752 233521,
Fax: +44 1752 233520,
Email : nrg@jack.see.plym.ac.uk

Key words: Vulnerability analysis, intrusion detection, intrusion response

Abstract: Addressing security vulnerabilities and system intrusions can represent a significant administrative overhead in current computer systems. Although technologies exist for both vulnerability scanning and for intrusion detection, the problems typically require some form of human intervention before they can be rectified. Evidence suggests that, in many cases, this can lead to omissions or oversights in terms of protection, as administrators are forced to prioritise their attention to security amongst various other tasks (particularly within smaller organisations, where a dedicated security administration function is unlikely to be found). As a result, mechanisms for automated response to the issues are considered to be advantageous. The paper describes the problems associated with vulnerability analysis and intrusion response, and then proceeds to consider how, at a conceptual level, the issues could be addressed within the framework of a wider architecture for intrusion monitoring.

1.   INTRODUCTION

The widespread use of Internet systems by organisations of all types means that the problem of IT security has never been more prominent. It would be no exaggeration to say that many organisations and individuals are reliant upon these systems, their correct operation and the data they contain. Despite their critical role, however, evidence has shown that systems are often vulnerable to various forms of abuse – breaching their security and resulting in intrusions. The problem of security breaches has substantially increased in recent years. In the CSI/FBI 2000 Computer Crime and Security Survey, financial losses due to computer security breaches mounted to $377,828,700, while the average annual total over the three years prior to 2000 was $120,240,180 [1].

An *intrusion* is the series of actions taken by an attacker against a target to achieve an unauthorised result. In order to fulfill this objective, the attacker must exploit a computer or network *vulnerability*, which represents the weakness of the system that allows unauthorised action to be taken [2]. For example, a well-known system vulnerability is the use of weak, default or even blank passwords [3]. These offer the opportunity for effortless access by attackers, who will routinely attempt to gain access to systems by trying default passwords, and then easily guessable ones. Only if these are unsuccessful will they need to resort to more sophisticated methods. Once inside, attackers can exploit other widely known vulnerabilities to increase their access (e.g. to attain root / administrator privileges).

This paper considers the dual problems of addressing security vulnerabilities and responding to intrusions that may result from their exploitation. In current systems, both elements can be seen to represent an administrative burden, with responsibility falling to system administration staff. In many cases, this may lead to omissions and prioritisation problems, as the same staff will often have numerous other responsibilities. It is considered that this issue is likely to be particularly acute within smaller organisations, due to the typical lack of dedicated IT security management staff. The discussion begins with an examination of the administrative problems posed by security vulnerabilities, in terms of the efforts required to identify and resolve an ever-increasing range of known problems. It then proceeds to consider the further considerations involved if it becomes necessary to respond to a suspected intrusion incident – which will often result from the exploitation of a vulnerability. The desirability of automated responses is recognised in both cases, leading to consideration of how an automated framework could be used to reduce the burden upon system administrators.

2. THE ADMINISTRATIVE PROBLEM OF SECURITY VULNERABILITIES

It is recognised that responding to both security vulnerabilities and detected intrusions can represent a significant administrative overhead. In the case of vulnerabilities, for example, there are associated overheads at two levels:

a) ensuring awareness of vulnerability existence;
b) being able to take appropriate corrective action to resolve them (e.g. installing software upgrades and patches).

Even though many exploits are based upon vulnerabilities that have been known for some time, the problem is a difficult one to keep on top of. Many software developers routinely release patches that enable known bugs and vulnerabilities in their products to be rectified – in some cases this happens before particular weaknesses have become publicly known, whilst in others it is in response to a problem being reported. As a result, the situation in many cases is that simple maintenance activity by system administrators is all that would be required to plug the holes. However, despite this, the problems clearly remain. The SANS Institute has identified several reasons why this may be the case [4]:

− 1.2 million new computers are added to the Internet every month;
− there is a lack of security experts to address the problems;
− the number of vulnerabilities continues to grow and there is no priority list for dealing with them.

From the system administrator's perspective, the main requirement is to ensure that the system remains operational and available – this is what the users expect and complaints will quickly occur if this is not the case. So, unless installing a patch is explicitly required to ensure that this is the case, then the task is likely to be given a lower priority.

Looking at the number of warnings that are issued, it is easy to see how administrators might downgrade the importance of responding to them immediately. This can be illustrated by considering the security bulletins issued by Microsoft Corporation in relation to its product range. When vulnerabilities are identified in Microsoft products, the company works to develop a solution and then issues an advisory bulletin when a software patch or upgrade is available for download. The graph in *Figure 1* summarises the number of security bulletins issued per month, between January 1999 and September 2000 (statistics obtained from http://www.microsoft.com/technet/security/current.asp).

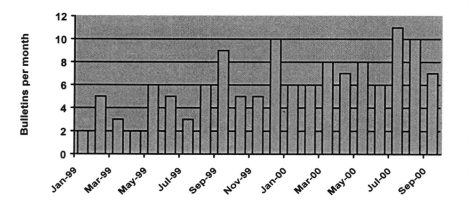

Figure 1. Microsoft Security Bulletins (January 1999 to September 2000)

It can be seen from the graph that the number of security bulletins issued ranges from two per month up to eleven per month (the average was 6 per month over the 21 month period). This might not be so bad if the associated patch was being installed on just a single system, but in some cases an organisation's IT and network configuration may dictate that the administrator must go around and update a number of individual systems in turn (which could obviously become quite time consuming). In some cases, the number of systems may run into the thousands, whereas the administration team may number less than ten. Relating this to the number of patches released per month, this could lead to each administrator having to patch about 20 machines per day (assuming the average of 6 patches per month and that all systems required them). It should also be remembered that these bulletins are only those related to Microsoft products. Where an organisation's IT set up is based upon a heterogeneous, multi-vendor configuration, security advisories from other sources would also have to be taken into consideration.

So, in view of all this, it can be appreciated that administrators might start out with good intentions, responding to each advisory as it arrives. However, this could quickly become burdensome and so the decision may be taken to batch them up and respond to them on a less frequent basis. Whilst this makes good administrative sense, it is less sensible from a security perspective. Once an advisory has been issued, the information about the associated vulnerability is available to anyone – and any hackers who were not aware of it before will certainly have access to it from then on. As such, any systems in which the weakness has not been addressed are exposed to a greater level of risk than before the advisory was made.

So what is the effect of not installing the available fixes? According to Attrition.org, 99% of the 5,823 web site defacements that occurred during 2000 were as a result of failure to patch known vulnerabilities for which the fixes were already available [5].

3.   INTRUSION RESPONSE

If a vulnerability is successfully exploited, a system intrusion is likely to result – which will require some form of consequent response. From this perspective, the issues of vulnerability analysis and intrusion response are related areas, separated only by the occurrence of an incident.

Intrusion response can be specified as the process of counteracting the effects of an intrusion. It includes the series of actions taken by an Intrusion Detection System, which follow the detection of a security-related event. It is important to note that consideration is not only given to taking action after an intrusion has been detected, but also when events of interest take place and raise the alert level of the system. That is the early stages of an attack, when the system is suspecting the occurrence of an intrusion, but is not yet confident enough.

It is possible to distinguish two main approaches to intrusion response, namely human/organisational approaches and technical methods.   The former are those that involve human processes and organisational structures, and may include actions such as reporting an incident to the police or invoking disciplinary procedures (e.g. in cases where internal personnel are responsible). By contrast, technical responses involve the use of functional techniques and software-based methods.   These technical actions can themselves be further sub-classified, into either passive or active forms of response [6]:

- **Passive responses**: aim to notify other parties (administrators - users) about the occurrence of an incident, relying on them to take further actions about it. Alarms, notifications and SNMP Traps are the most common passive responses. Passive actions are the most common response options in commercial IDS systems.
- **Active responses**: are the actions taken by a process or system to encounter the incident that has occurred. Those actions might include collecting more information about the incident, limiting permitted user behaviour, or blocking IP traffic through firewalls and routers.

Within these categories there are myriad individual response actions that could be pursued and some decision making ability is required when a suspected incident presents itself. However, although the type of incident will suggest a range of possible responses, the classification of incident alone does not provide enough information to determine which one(s) are actually appropriate. The *specific* response(s) to initiate will depend upon a number of factors, which collectively identify the context in which the incident has occurred. This idea is illustrated in *Figure 2*.

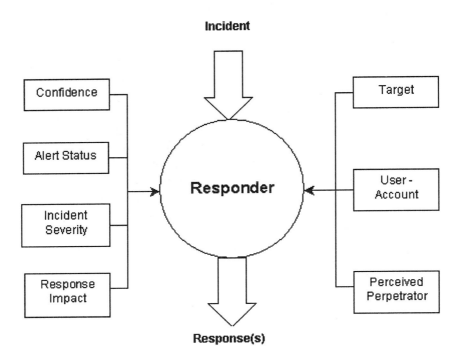

Figure 2. Factors influencing intrusion response

As the diagram shows, the *incident* is the trigger for the response and still represents the principal influence over what should be done. However, the other influencing factors that also need to be considered are as follows:

- **Confidence:** how many monitored characteristics within the system are suggestive of an intrusion having occurred?
- **Alert status:** what is the current status of the monitoring system, both on the suspect account / process and in the system overall?
- **Incident severity:** what impact has the incident already had upon the confidentiality, integrity or availability of the system and its data? How strong a response is required at this stage?

- **Response impact:** what would be the impact of initiating a particular form of response? How would it affect a legitimate user if the suspected intrusion was, in fact a false alarm? Would there be any adverse impacts upon other system users if a particular response action were taken?
- **Target:** what system, resource or data appears to be the focus of the attack. What assets are at risk if the incident continues or is able to be repeated?
- **User account:** if the attack is being conducted through the suspected compromise of a user account, what privileges are associated with that account?
- **Perceived perpetrator:** does the evidence collected suggest that the perpetrator is an external party or an insider?

At the heart of *Figure 2* was an entity referred to as the *responder*. This is the element that will assess the various factors in order to select and invoke the required response(s). Although a great deal of work has been done in the area of automated intrusion detection, current systems are able to do very little in terms of automated response when they suspect a problem. So, in current systems, the responder role is likely to be taken by a system administrator. However, there are practical limits to the effectiveness of this approach. Firstly, the administration of increasingly large and complicated IT infrastructures becomes correspondingly more cumbersome. Secondly, the widespread use of automated scripts to generate attacks of a distributed nature [7] can render the speed of traditional response methods inadequate. As with vulnerability analysis and resolution, therefore, the administrative burden may again mean that the handling of intrusion response becomes sidelined - although, of course, there may be more incentive to respond to an intrusion because it represents a vulnerability that has already been exploited.

4.   AUTOMATED RESPONSE FRAMEWORKS

In order to assist in resolving the problem of administrative overhead, some form of automated response framework is desirable. For vulnerabilities, it can be observed that there are already numerous tools available to assist in the task of scanning systems to identify potential holes. However, this only goes part of the way to addressing the problem. It relieves the administrators of having to have the detailed knowledge of system security necessary to identify weaknesses, but it still requires their attention to both run an analysis and take consequent corrective actions.

Although some scanning software includes functionality for fixing problems identified, the current approaches are limited - minor system configuration weaknesses can be rectified, but many vulnerabilities require more substantial action than this.   Given that vulnerabilities and intrusions are linked issues, it makes sense for vulnerability analysis and resolution to form part of an overall intrusion monitoring approach.

Figure 3 illustrates the conceptual architecture of the Intrusion Monitoring System (IMS), a research prototype that the authors are currently developing.   IMS is an architecture for intrusion monitoring and activity supervision, based around the concept of a centralised host handling the monitoring of a number of networked client systems.   Intrusion detection in the system is based upon the comparison of current user activity against both historical profiles of 'normal' behaviour for legitimate users and intrusion specifications of recognised attack patterns.   The architecture is comprised of a number of functional modules, addressing data collection and response on the client side and data analysis and recording at the host.

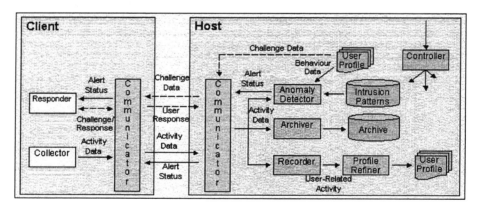

Figure 3. The Intrusion Monitoring System architecture

The full architecture is described in [8] but, from the perspective of the current discussion, the relevant modules are the *Collector, Anomaly Detector* and *Responder* – which can be used to perform activity monitoring (to identify intrusions) and vulnerability scanning, as well as appropriate follow-up actions in the event of problems.

The *Collector* is responsible for obtaining information from individual monitored client systems.   In terms of activity monitoring, this information may relate to user data such as applications and files accessed, keystroke data (for biometric analysis) and resource usage statistics.   From the perspective of vulnerability scanning, the *Collector* could also take on the role of obtaining system configuration details and the like, which would then be sent for subsequent analysis.

The *Anomaly Detector* resides on the host side and is the main recipient of the *Collector's* data. For user activity, it compares the information against historical profiles of 'normal' behaviour (e.g. frequently used applications, typing style) to identify anomalies that may indicate either an impostor or misuse by a legitimate user. In addition, generic intrusion specifications will be used to compare activities against known patterns of misuse – with a match triggering some form of alert.   From a vulnerability analysis perspective, the *Anomaly Detector* will compare the collected scan data against a database of known weaknesses.   In the event of problems, the *Anomaly Detector* will increase the alert status of the monitoring system and interact with the *Responder* module.

The *Responder* provides an automated facility for dealing with suspected problems. There are numerous forms of response that it would be possible to allow a system to initiate under automatic control. A small selection of ideas are listed below:

– further investigation of the incident via data collected in audit log files;
– increasing the level monitoring and/or auditing;
– issuing a challenge for further authentication;
– limiting permitted user behaviour;
– delaying (or lowering priority of) intruder's session / process;
– termination (or suspension) of the anomalous session / process.

It is the *Responder* that would be responsible for assessing and weighting the contextual factors that would determine the appropriate response option(s) for a given incident occurrence. As such, the *Responder* (like the *Anomaly Detector*) requires an element of intelligent analysis and decision-making.

In the vulnerability analysis context, the decision about what to do is potentially clear-cut, but the issue remains about when to do it.   The *Responder* could conceivably take the role of coordinating and conducting updates on the affected client systems in order to resolve problems identified. A library of fixes, updates and patches would be accumulated and maintained on the host side and then issued to clients as necessary.

The description presented here proposes the solution at a conceptual level only. In practice, of course, the associated mechanisms would be far more involved and elements represented as single boxes or flows within *Figure 3* would potentially be realised as a large number of sub-processes. Some issues, such as how the system can maintain awareness of new vulnerabilities and acquire associated patches, remain unresolved and require further investigation. Other aspects, such as the anomaly detection methods and response framework, are already the focus of active research.

5.   CONCLUSIONS

Automated response approaches such as those described have the potential to significantly reduce the burden on system administrators. Indeed, within the framework of an approach such as that proposed with IMS, the whole process of intrusion prevention, detection, response and resolution could be addressed.

Although the proposed approaches have the advantages identified, it is recognised that there is also a risk that any automated action taken could be incorrect.   In the case of vulnerabilities, attempts to rectify security weaknesses or install software patches on the fly could adversely affect the operation of the system and/or cause incompatibility with existing elements. In the case of intrusion response, the automatic invocation of an inappropriate method could result in insufficient action being taken or, alternatively, could interrupt or deny service to a legitimate activity.   As such, both are aspects that require careful configuration and their degree of permitted autonomy would strongly depend upon the nature of the system they were protecting.

The design of the automated response frameworks is the focus of ongoing research by the authors.   Further details of the associated architectural approaches and implementation experiences will be reported in future publications.

6.   REFERENCES

[1]   CSI. 2001. "Financial losses due to Internet intrusions, trade secret theft and other cyber crimes soar", CSI Press Release, 12 March 2001. http://www.gocsi.com/prelea_000321.htm

[2]   Howard, J. 1997. "An Analysis of Security Incidents on the Internet 1989 – 1995", PhD thesis. Carnegie Mellon University, April 1997. http://www.cert.org/research/JHThesis

[3]   SANS Institute. 2001. "How To Eliminate The Ten Most Critical Internet Security Threats. The Experts' Consensus", Version 1.32, 18 January 2001. http://www.sans.org/topten.htm.

[4]   Noack, D. 2000.   "The Back Door Into Cyber-Terrorism", APBnews.com Report, 2 June 2000.

[5]   CNET. 2001. "Patchwork Security - Software "fixes" routinely available but often ignored", CNET News.com report.   24 January 2001. http://news.cnet.com/news/0-1007-201-4578373-0.html

[6]   Bace, R. and Mell, P. 2001.   "NIST Special Publication on Intrusion Detection Systems", National Institute of Standards and Technology (NIST),   http://csrc.nist.gov/publications/drafts/idsdraft.pdf,   February 12 2001.

[7]   Cheung, S. and Levitt, K.N. 1997. "Protecting Routing Infrastructures from Denial of Service Using Cooperative Intrusion Detection", Proceedings   of   the   New   Security   Paradigms   Workshop, Langdale,Cumbria   UK,   September   23   -   26,   1997, http://riss.keris.or.kr:8080/pubs/contents/proceedings/commsec/28369 9/

[8]   Furnell, S.M. and Dowland, P.S. 2000. "A conceptual architecture for real-time   intrusion   monitoring",   *Information   Management   &   Computer Security*, Vol. 8, No. 2, pp65-74.

A NEW PARADIGM FOR ADDING SECURITY INTO IS DEVELOPMENT METHODS

MIKKO SIPONEN[a] AND RICHARD BASKERVILLE[b]

[a] *University of Oulu, Department of Information Processing Science, P.O. BOX 3000, 90014 Oulu Oulu, Finland, Mikko.T.siponen@oulu.fi*

[b] *Georgia State University, 35 Broad Street, Atlanta, Georgia 30031, baskerville@gsu.edu*

Abstract: Information system (IS) development methods pay little attention to security aspects. Consequently, several alternative approaches for designing and managing secure information systems (SIS) have been proposed. However, many of these approaches have shortcomings. These approaches lack fully comprehensive modeling schemes in terms of security, i.e. no single method covers all modeling needs. Rarely can these approaches be integrated into existing IS development methods. Also, these approaches do not facilitate the autonomy of developers. This paper describes a framework that helps us understand the fundamental barriers preventing the alternative SIS design approaches from more effectively addressing these shortcomings. This framework is illustrated with an example of a framework-based solution: meta-notation for adding security into IS development methods. Future research questions and implications for research and practice are presented.

Key words: IS security

1.   INTRODUCTION

IS and computer science literatures are rife with the importance of security considerations for IS organizations (e.g. Anderson, 1999;

Backhouse & Dhillon, 2001; Straub & Welke, 1998). The exploding use of the Internet by different organizations and the general public has led to 'security' becoming a recognised public buzzword. As a result, a huge number of technical solutions exist in the area of computer and communication security. However, technical solutions do not provide much help from the viewpoint of IS and Management Information Systems (MIS); for example, such solutions do not help to design or manage secure IS (Baskerville, 1989; Sandhu & Thomas, 1994; Baskerville, 1993; Backhouse & Dhillon, 2001). Furthermore, the methods for developing IS do not give much help with respect to security issues (Baskerville, 1993; Dhillon & Backhouse, 2001). Various security design approaches (ranging from simple checklists to more advanced approaches modified from IS and software development methods) have been expounded by practitioners and researchers. Table 1 summarizes the existing approaches/paradigms for design and managing secure IS.

Table 1. The different approaches for information security management IS security design.

The different paradigms	Examples/advocates	Key ideas/arguments
Mainstream Approaches		
Checklists/standard	BS 7799 (1993); GASSP (1999); ITSEC (1990); OECD (1996); Wood et al. (1987)	List the ideal protection means that organizations should implement
Risk Management	Wong (1977); Custance (1996); Bennett & Kailay (1992); Freeman et al. (1997); Spruit & Samwel (1999) Jung et al. (1999)	Calculate occurrence of risks and the justification of controls
Formal development	Anderson (1993); Barnes (1998)	Formalization is key for achieving security.
Self-reflected security management cookbooks	Parker (1981; 1998); Perry (1985); Schwaitzer (1984); Warman (1993).	Each author presents his/her own principles for security management. The use of risk management and checklists-orientation are common to these approaches
Integrative Approaches		
Information/Data Base modeling approaches	Smith (1989); Ellmer et al. (1995); Pernul et al. (1998)	Modeling notations for expressing security constraints based on structural and object-oriented paradigms
Responsibility approaches	Dhillon & Backhouse (1996); McDermott & Fox (1999)	Identification of workers' role responsibilities is key for designing security in organizations

Business process	Herrmann & Pernul (1999), Röhm et al. (1998); Röhm and Pernul (1998; 1999)	Add security constraints in the business processes
The security-modified IS development approaches	Baskerville (1998); Booysen & Eloff (1995); Hitchings (1995, 1996); James (1996)	These security approaches are influenced by different IS development methods

For a closer look at these approaches, readers are referred to (Baskerville, 1993; Dhillon & Backhouse, 2001; Siponen, 2001).

BARRIERS TO MAINSTREAM APPROACHES

The mainstream methods include checklists/standards, risk management, formal development and self-reflected cookbooks. Checklists/standards (Eloff & Solms, 2000; Fitzgerald, 1995; Janczewski, 2000; Solms, 1997, 1998, 1999) - have at least three fundamental roadblocks that are problematic.

First and foremost, the driven IS security development paradigm of checklists/standards methods have been based on "what can be done" by means of available solutions (Baskerville, 1993). In the case of checklists, this means that the unique needs and problems of organizations are overlooked (e.g. Baskerville, 1988; 1993). The needs of organizations are replaced by ideal protection techniques based on the intuitions of security gurus', and organizations are required to follow these as "a gift from the Heaven". Furthermore, when practitioners applying checklists/standards are confronted with any management decision-making questions, they have to play it by ear. For these reasons, the real developmental or management support of these methods remains very weak.

Secondly, checklists/standards, risk management and formal development, being stand-alone/separated methods, are confronted with the problem of developmental duality, meaning that security and IS developments are separate activities having conflicting requirements (Baskerville, 1994).

Thirdly, these techniques (checklists and formal method development) are necessarily mechanistic and functionalistic and therefore conflict with the modern view of the social nature of organizations (Dhillon & Backhouse, 2001). In the case of checklists, this is perhaps due to the fact that the mainstream academic research on security is focused on technical matters, and since checklists simply attempt to reflect state-of-the-art research, the help checklists offer remains very mechanistic. Formal methods, owing to the engineering viewpoint of development, focus only on technical aspects of development. Also several books on security management exist, presenting less systematic cookbook approaches, based on the author's own personal experiences and speculations. It is typical for these books that the authors are highly self-reflective, i.e. they do not bother to take into account what others have done in the field nor have they carried out empirical studies (hence, the label self-reflected security management cookbooks).

Blocked by these barriers, these approaches have had only limited success for designing and managing secure IS (Dhillon & Backhouse, 2001).

BARRIERS TO INTEGRATIVE APPROACHES

To avoid the shortcomings of these mainstream methods (checklists, risk management, formalization and cookbooks), more integrative approaches have been developed that integrate security design more closely with the social organization, the essential information system design, or the organizational goals. These approaches do not seem to have received wide attention. In Table 1, these approaches are classified in terms of different paradigms: information modeling, responsibility, business process, the security-modified IS development approaches, according to (Siponen, 2001). Even though these advanced approaches improved security management/design considerably (e.g. paying attention to organizations' security requirements), they engender their own set of barriers.

Firstly, these approaches lack a comprehensive modeling support in terms of security (Siponen, 2001). In other words, three levels of modeling/abstraction for an IS is widely recognized: organizational, conceptual and technical level (Iivari & Koskela, 1987; Iivari, 1989; Lyytinen, 1987). The different IS security approaches cover the different levels of IS, but no single method provide a comprehensive modeling support (e.g. for all three levels: organizational, conceptual and technical level).

Secondly, the existing approaches apart from Baskerville (1988; 1989), Booysen & Eloff (1995); James (1996) and McDermott & Fox (1999), are difficult – even impossible - to integrate into IS or software development process. This results in the problem of developmental duality (cf. Baskerville, 1992). Developmental duality is a fundamental conflict between the functionality (designed into the basic information system by business systems analysts) with the security (designed and added by security systems analysts).

Thirdly, the existing approaches restrict the autonomy of developers to use the approaches they prefer. Developers are increasingly recognized for their practice of using a "toolkit" of methods and method fragments, and selecting these according to the situation (Kumar & Welke, 1992). They may choose universal modeling for one project, and extreme programming for the next, according to the problem setting. If developers want to address security aspects into IS development using the existing security methods, they are not only forced to abandon their existing IS development methods, but also their practice of autonomously selecting the methods they desire.

Fourthly, IS methods are known to be emergent (Truex et al., 1999). New methods spring up every now and then, and methods are never really executed in practice exactly the same way (Truex et al., 2000). It is difficult to predict this emergence, and to allow for a universal security method that will match every development method and its permutations. Our goal should be to integrate security into each (existing, forthcoming and unpredictable) IS development method. However given the trend of current security methods, security approaches would, at best, always come a few steps behind IS development methods. The more rapidly the development evolution, the farther behind are the security approaches.

A NEW PARADIGM: OVERCOMING THE BARRIERS

From the problem framework above, it becomes clear that a meta-level viewpoint could provide one solution. Rather than present yet another new method with its own novel security features, we propose that security approaches must rise a level of abstraction above the barriers. Moving a level away from methodology takes us into the realm of meta-methodology, which will help developers use and modify our existing methods as needed.

Meta-methodology is not a well-explored area. Much of the work to date has focussed on method engineering (Brinkkemper, et al 1996; Kumar & Welke, 1992), and formalisms to support computer-aided method engineering (Odell, 1996). Such computer-based meta-methods essentially provide the means for rapidly (almost instantly) developing computer-aided systems analysis and software engineering (CASA/CASE) tools to match development needs and settings. While the security imperative for such meta-methods has been declared (Baskerville, 1996), there is little formal work in security meta-methodology.

Developing a full security meta-methodology is beyond the scope of a single paper. However, to illustrate the feasibility and the need for the solution that proceeds from this framework, a method fragment will suffice. This paper will describe a meta-notation, a key feature of most methods and meta-methods. The remainder of this study is organized as follows. The second section discusses the background of the meta-notation. In the third section, the meta-notation is explicated along with an exemplification. The fourth section is a discussion of the issues raised, and it is followed by a conclusion where the contributions of the paper are summarized.

2.   PATTERNS IN IS DEVELOPMENT AND SECURITY METHOD NOTATION

Moving to a meta-method level of abstraction yields a perspective of information systems design methods that are in a constant state of emergence and change. No systems problem setting is an exact repeat of a former setting, and no method can actually be applied exactly the same way every time. This thesis is well known in practice (Jaaksi, 1998), and has been shown empirically and logically in academe (Truex et al., 2000). Neither however, are systems problem settings and development approaches total chaos and relativism. Otherwise, practical and empirical experience would have no value. Instead developers recognize regularities or patterns in the way problem settings arise and methods emerge. A comprehensive meta-methodology must apprehend a sufficient range of these patterns in order to be useful.

SUBJECTS AND OBJECTS

In seeking patterns in systems development methods, notation systems quickly rise in their apparent regularity across methods and problem settings. Traditionally IS development methods help developers to understand and model reality with respect to the system-to-be-built. In order to do such analysis and modeling, developers need to agree on how to describe things. Traditionally things are classified as 'entities' (e.g. structural methods) or 'objects' (e.g. object-oriented methods) in the IS literature. Additionally, some approaches uses 'Actors' (e.g. UML type of use case) or 'stickfigures' (e.g. Checkland's rich picture) at the organizational level (e.g. requirements analysis stage) as a unit of analysis. In our schema, the 'entities' or 'objects' are classified as security subjects and objects. As a result, these notational dimensions can, in principle, be added into any of the many notational patterns that use entities or objects as units of analysis. For example, both the structural and object-oriented forms of information engineering methods (cf. Lyytinen, 1987) are good candidates for the addition of such security notation.

The terms security subjects and objects are commonly used in database security literature to describe computer access control policies and models (e.g. Castano et al. 1995; Foley, 1991; McLean, 1990; Sandhu, 1993; Summers, 1997). Common security classification schemes are in turn influenced by these computer access control policies and models from the field of database security.

CONSTRAINTS

In the security literature, there is wide agreement on three security requirements (Parker, 1998): confidentiality or non-disclosure (prevent/detect improper disclosure of information), integrity (information should not be modified by unauthorized personnel), availability (information should only be available to authorized personnel). In addition to these three requirements, the need for "non-repudiation" has been recently recognized. Non-repudiation is important for enabling financial transactions and data interchange key to electronic commerce. It is needed to make valid large-scale contracts between vendors and customers. Non-repudiation means that a contracting party cannot subsequently deny their actions. These four security requirements are called security constraints. While some computer security researchers, particularly cryptographers, distinguish other security requirements (see e.g. Menezes et al., 1997), the four described here are sufficient for our purposes to capture most of the common patterns found in security and systems development. Additional requirements can certainly be added to the meta-notation on an ad-hoc basis as required.

3. META-NOTATION SEMANTICS

The meta-notation includes five dimensions: security subjects, security objects, security constraints, security classifications, and security policy. The security classification (e.g., "secret," "top secret" etc.) can be regarded as more optional than the other dimensions (see below). Security subjects denote the different security relevant entities, i.e. entities that have a relevant security connection to the assets of the organization (security objects). Security subjects may include employees of the organization, business partners and third-parties. Actors in use cases and stickfigures in rich pictures, given that they have a security relevant connection to the assets of the organizations, are security subjects. The term security objects refers to the assets of the organization that are of relevance in terms of information security. Such assets (security objects) may range from physical things such as paper to electronic entities such as files. Security constraints include confidentiality, integrity, availability and non-repudiation. In order to define the kind of access (e.g. read, write, etc.) to objects that subjects need, a security classification of the security objects and security subjects may be relevant. If this is the case, subjects are classified according to their security sensitivity/need. Herein security policy dimension defines other constraints that may apply to security subjects (see the example below).

3.1   An example of the use of meta-notation

In the following example, the meta-notation (five security dimensions: security subjects, security objects, security constraints, security classifications, and security policy) is applied into a use case notation. Most object-oriented methods employ 'use cases' in requirements analysis phase to collect and analyze requirements (Jaaksi, 1998). Use case demonstrates what a user should be able to do with the system; use cases are graphical or textual presentation of the usage of system (Jaaksi, 1998). "when a user uses the system, she or he will perform a behaviorally related sequence of transactions in a dialogue with the system. We call such a special sequence as use case" (Jacobson et al., 1992). Figure 2 illustrates a traditional textual use case description (the template is modified from Jaaksi, 1998). The use case is 'booking' (Figure 2: Booking). Presume a 'use case' where a clerk works in a travel agency (Figure 2: actor). The booking clerk books journeys for different customers (Figure 2: functional summary). Such booking occurs several times a day (Figure 2: frequency) and booking or query to database should take less than 30 seconds (Figure 2: usability requirements). In order to do such 'booking', the booking clerk needs to access to the booking database/file, and the customer file.

Use case: Booking.

Version: 1.0

Functional Summary: A booking clerk books journeys for customers.

Frequency: several times a day

Usability requirements: Any database query and booking must be able to carry out in less than 30 seconds.

Actor: a clerk.

Preconditions: Preconditions: Booking and customer databases exist.

Exceptions: If information on certain journey is not available an appropriate error message is produced.

Figure 2. A traditional use case.

Now presume that security considerations are wanted to address in systems development (including this use case). Figure 3 describes the use case presented in figure 2 enriched by five security dimensions (meta-notation).

Use case: Booking.
Version: 1.0
Functional Summary: A booking clerk books journeys for customers.
Frequency: several times a day
Usability requirements: Any database query and booking must be able to carry out in less than 30 seconds.
Actor/security subject: A clerk
Security classification: confidential
Security objects and access types to security objects: object 11: customer file (the clerk must be able to read, write and delete the customer information); object 15: booking database (the clerk must be able to read, write and delete the customer information on the database)
Security policy/Specific security restrictions: the clerk is only allowed to access security objects classified as confidential with the booking department.
Preconditions: Booking and customer databases exist. The identity of the booking clerk/security subject has been validated.
Exceptions: If information on certain journey is not available an appropriate error message is produced.

Figure 3. A security enriched use case.

In figure 3, five security dimensions (security subjects, security classification, access to objects, security constraint, security policy) are added to the use case. In the use case 'booking', the security subject is the booking clerk (Figure 3: Actor/security subject). In this example, the clerk's security classification is confidential (Figure 3: security classifications: classification of security subjects). Presume that the relevant security objects with respect to this use case are objects 11 (the customer file) and 15 (the booking database) – figure 3: Security objects. The types of access to these objects are read, write/delete/update (Figure 3: The types of access to the security objects). This is because in this example/use case, the booking clerk must be able to read and update (write, delete) to these objects. Presume that is specified in a security policy that the booking clerks can only access to objects labeled as confidential within the booking department. This security policy requirement is expressed in the security enriched use case (Figure 3: Security policy/Specific security restrictions).

4.   DISCUSSION AND IMPLICATIONS

The existing SIS design approaches lack a comprehensive modeling support. The different IS security approaches cover the different levels of IS, but no single method provide a comprehensive modeling support. Yet, many of the existing approaches can not be integrated into IS or software development methods. This is problem as termed as the problem of developmental duality (cf. Baskerville, 1992). Moreover, the existing approaches restrict the autonomy of developers to use the approaches they prefer. Finally, IS development methods are known to be emergent and evolving (Truex et al. 1999): novel methods arise every now and then, and are modified by practitioners to fit different situations (Jaaksi, 1998). However, it is difficult to put forth one universal security method that will match every existing, forthcoming and unpredictable IS development methods and they permutations. It is argued a meta-level viewpoint is one solution to address the aforementioned concerns.

With respect to the problem concerning a lack of comprehensive modeling support by existing single methods, this paper proposes a meta-notation which provides modeling support for different levels of IS. The same goes for the lack of methodological support for security aspects of web-IS.

The solution avoids the problem of developmental duality. This meta-notation can be added to the any existing notation for modeling IS or software. Given that one wants to avoid the problem of developmental duality, it is impossible to provide security specific notation (excluding the meta-notation that can be applied to different, if not all, existing modeling notations). Security specific notation would inevitably lead to the problem of developmental duality. Such security specific notation cannot be used to model normal IS development, as security development and normal IS or software development would be carried out using different methods. However, any introduction of a new method, which includes both normal and security development, would restrict the autonomy of developers to use the approaches they prefer (they would have to use this particular approach and in all likelihood abandon their "old" methods/practices). This proposed solution facilitates the developers autonomy: developers can use the methods they prefer as a basis of development.

IMPLICATIONS FOR RESEARCH

This paper has suggested a new paradigm for addressing security aspects in IS development. This new paradigm proposed that, in order to integrate security smoothly into IS development processes, we should move a level away from methodology - such as into the domain of meta-methodology.

Yet, by adapting such a meta-view, the proposed approach has shown a new direction to pay attention to developers' autonomy. The possibility to maximize the use of developer's preferred IS development methods may avoid such problems as the ever increasing cost of system development (e.g. Necco et al, 1987) and lack of developer's satisfaction with respect to the methods used (Mahmood, 1987). However, future research is needed to increase our understanding of the usability and implications of this approach. Empirical research is needed to explore the applicability of this approach to practice. Yet, future research should study can this approach, by facilitating developers' autonomy, improve the developers' motivation with respect to methods.

IMPLICATIONS FOR PRACTICE

As for practitioners, the proposed meta-notation (five dimensions) ensures that security issues are addressed properly and easily in IS and software development. Yet, this proposal satisfies the requirements of autonomy better than any existing methods for designing secure IS. Practitioners can continue to use their favored IS development methods as a basis for the development/management of secure IS.

5.   CONCLUSIONS

Information system development methods do not address security aspects seriously enough. As a result, several SIS design and management approaches, from checklists to more advanced endeavors reflecting IS development, are put forth. However, these approaches have a few weaknesses. The different SIS design approaches cover the different levels of IS, but lack the comprehensiveness needed. Most of the approaches for designing SIS are difficult to integrate into IS development methods. Moreover, existing SIS design approaches do not assist the autonomy of developers. This paper considered a framework describing barriers preventing the alternative SIS design approaches from more effectively addressing these lapses. Based on this framework, a meta-notation, for adding security into IS development methods, was presented. Finally, implications for research and practice were presented.

ACKNOWLEDGEMENTS

This research was supported by a research grant by University of Oulu (Finland), and also financed by OWLA-project (http://www.hytec.oulu.fi/).

This paper has been written while Mikko Siponen has been with the Department of Computer Information Systems, J. Mack Robinson College of Business, Georgia State University, Georgia, USA.

6. REFERENCES

Anderson, R., (1999), How to Cheat at the Lottery (or, Massively Parallel Requirements Engineering), Annual Computer Security Applications Conference (ACSAC99).

Baskerville, R., (1988), Designing Information Systems Security. John Wiley Information Systems Series.

Baskerville, R., (1989), Logical Controls Specification: An approach to information system security", In H. Klein & K. Kumar (eds.) systems development for human progress. Amsterdam: North-Holland.

Baskerville, R., (1993), Information Systems Security Design Methods: Implications for Information Systems Development. ACM Computing Surveys 25, (4) December, pp. 375-414.

Baskerville, R. (1996). Structural Artifacts in Method Engineering: The Security Imperative. In S. Brinkkemper & K. Lyytinen & R. Welke (Eds.), Method Engineering (pp. 8-28). London: Chapman & Hall.

Booysen, H.A.S., & Eloff, J.H.P., (1995), A Methodology for the development of secure Application Systems. In proceeding of the 11th IFIP TC11 international conference on information security, IFIP/SEC'95.

Brinkkemper, S., Lyytinen, K., & Welke, R. (Eds.). (1996). Method Engineering. London: Chapman & Hall.

Castano, S., Fugini, M., Martell, G., & Samarati, P., (1995), Database Security. Addison-Wesley.

Code of Practice for Information Security Management, (1993), Department of Trade and Industry. DISC PD003. British Standard Institution, London, UK.

Dhillon, G. and Backhouse, J., (2001), Current directions in IS security research: toward socio-organizational perspectives. Information Systems Journal. Vol 11, No 2.

Ellmer, E., Pernul, G., Kappel, G., (1995), Object-Oriented Modeling of Security Semantics. In: Proceedings of the 11th Annual Computer Society Applications Conference (ACSAC'95). IEEE Computer Society Press.

Foley, S.N., (1991), A Taxonomy for Information Flow Policies and Models. Proceedings of the 1991 IEEE Computer Security Symposium on Research in Security and Privacy.

Hirschheim, R., Klein, H. K., & Lyytinen, K., (1995), Information Systems Development and Data Modelling: Conceptual and Philosophical Foundations. Cambridge University Press, UK.

Hitchings, J., (1995), Achieving an Integrated Design: The Way forward for Information Security. Proceedings of the IFIP TC11 eleventh international conference on information security, IFIP/SEC'95.

Hitchings, J., (1996), A Practical solution to the complex human issues of information security design. Proceedings of the 12th IFIP TC11 international conference on information security, IFIP/SEC'96.

Iivari, J., (1989), Levels of abstraction as a Conceptual Framework for an Information Systems. In E. D. Falkenberg and P. Lindgreen (eds): Information System Concepts: An In-depth Analysis. North-Holland, Amsterdam.

Iivari, J & Koskela, E., (1987), The PIOCO model for IS design, MIS Quarterly, Vol. 11, No. 3, pp. 401-419.

Jaaksi, A., (1998), Our Cases with Use Cases. Journal of Object-Oriented Programming, vol. 10, no. 9, pp. 58-65.

Jacobson, I., Christerson, P. Jonsson, P., Övergaard, G., (1992), A Use Case Driven Approach. Addison-Wesley Publishing Company.

James, H.L., (1996), Managing information systems security: a soft approach. Proceedings of the Information Systems Conference of New Zealand. IEEE Society Press.

Kumar, K. & Welke, R.J., (1992), Methodology engineering: A Proposal for situation-specific Methodology construction. In W.W. Cotterman & J.A. Senn (eds): Challenges and Strategies for research in systems development, pp. 257-269.

Lyytinen, K., (1987), Two Views on Information Modeling. Information & Management, Vol. 12, pp. 9-19.

Lyytinen, K., (1991), A Taxonomic Perspective of Information Systems Development: Theoretical Constructs and Recommendations. In R.J. Boland & R.A. Hirscheim (ed): Critical Issues in Information Systems Research, John Wiley & Sons Ltd.

McDermott, J. & Fox, C., "Using abuse case models for security requirements", Proceedings of the 15th Annual Computer Security Applications Conference (ACSAC). IEEE Computer Society Press (1999).

McLean, J., (1990), The specification and modelling of computer security. IEEE Computer. January, vol. 23, issue 1, pp. 9-16.

Menezes, A.J., van Oorschot, P.C. and Vanstone, S.C., (1999), Handbook of Applied Cryptography. CRC Press, USA.

Odell, J. J. (1996). A primer to method engineering. In S. Brinkkkemper & K. Lyytinen & R. Welke (Eds.), Method Engineering: Principles of method construction and tool support (pp. 1-7). London: Chapman & Hall.

Parker, D. B., (1998), Fighting Computer Crime - A New Framework for Protecting Information. Wiley Computer Publishing. USA.

Pernul, G., Tjoa A. M., & Winiwarter, W., (1998), Modelling Data Secrecy and Integrity. Data & Knowledge Engineering. Vol. 26, pp. 291-308. North Holland.

Röhm, A.W., Pernul, G. & Herrmann, G., (1998), Modelling secure and fair electronic commerce. Proceedings of the 14th Annual Computer Security Applications Conference, 1998.

Röhm, A.W., Pernul, G., (1999), COPS: a model and infrastructure for secure and fair electronic markets. Proceedings of the 32nd Annual Hawaii International Conference on Systems Sciences (HICSS-32).

Sandhu, R.S., (1993), Lattice-based access controls. IEEE Computer. Vol. 26, no. 11, November, pp. 9-19.

Siponen, M.T., (2001), An analysis of the recent IS security development approaches: descriptive and prescriptive implications. In: G. Dhillon (eds:) Information Security Management - Global Challenges in the Next Millennium, Idea Group (2001).

Summers, R. C., (1997), Secure Computing: Treats and Safeguards. McGraw-Hill.

Straub, D.W. & Welke, R.J., (1998), Coping with Systems Risk: Security Planning Models for Management Decision Making. MIS Quarterly, Vol. 22, No. 4, p. 441-464.

Truex, D. P., Baskerville, R., & Klein, H. K. (1999). Growing Systems in an Emergent Organization. Communications of The ACM, 42(8), 117-123.

Truex, D., Baskerville, R., & Travis, J. (2000). Amethodical Systems Development: The Deferred Meaning of Systems Development Methods. Accounting, Management and Information Technology, 10, 53-79.

USING SOFT SYSTEMS METHODOLOGY TO FACILITATE THE DEVELOPMENT OF A COMPUTER SECURITY TEACHING MODULE

J. BIGGAM, A. HOGARTH

Department of Business Information Management,School of Business,Glasgow Caledonian University,Glasgow, SCOTLAND, UK

Telephone: (0141) 331 3943

Fax: (0141) 331 3193

E-Mail: J.Biggam@gcal.ac.uk, A.Hogarth@gcal.ac.uk

Key words: Computer Security, Computer Crime, Soft Systems Methodology, Requirements Engineering

Abstract: Computer security issues are now commonplace in the business community. Incidents such as computer viruses, Web vandalism, computer theft, etc. are regularly highlighted by the media. Indeed, the drive towards E-Business has raised the profile of security incidents. Many stakeholders play an important part in counteracting these security breaches, including law enforcement, the business community, hardware and software vendors, and researchers. The purpose of this paper is to highlight the role of universities in the battle against computer security breaches and to show, through a case study, how one university used the Soft Systems Methodology (SSM) to develop a computer security module for its undergraduate students.

1.   INTRODUCTION

What is meant by 'computer security'? Examples of computer security incidents are plentiful, ranging from computer hacking, the deliberate spread of computer viruses to computer fraud, theft and sabotage incidents. Similarly, there are a corresponding multitude of security countermeasures, including anti-virus software, firewalls, encryption tools and techniques, anti-theft devices, etc. (Biggam [1]; Gollmann [2]). The use of the Internet by the business community has raised the profile of computer security, with Web defacements by groups such as as "Prime Suspectz", "Insanity Zine", "Smoked Crew", "Crime Boys" and "Silver Lords" a thorn in the E-Business community (Martin [3]):

Figure 1. Web Site Example

Web Vandalism, viruses, computer-related fraud, laptop theft and the sabotage of file servers are all examples of computer crime. Surprisingly, in Scotland there is no legal definition of computer crime – indeed, there is no legal definition of what is meant by a "computer". Nonetheless, computer crime is tackled by the police through a number of laws. For instance, unauthorized access, the spread of viruses, and the intention to commit a further offense are covered within the Computer Misuse Act 1990. Although computer crime is legally undefined in Scotland, this lack of a definition is not seen as a hindrance to either understanding what is meant by such crime or to tackling those who target computers or use computers to commit a criminal act.

What is the extent of computer security breaches? This is not an easy question to answer, for a variety of reasons. The business community often prefer to deal with computer security internally, thus incidents often remain hidden from the police and the public. In one incident recently, a student telephoned a company to report a security vulnerability within the company's Web site, but rather than thank the student for highlighting this security issue, the company instead threatened legal action against the student. A recent survey (Computer Security Institute [4]) highlights that only 25% of respondents reported computer security issues to law enforcement.

In terms of gaining statistics, within Scotland there have been no surveys ascertaining the extent of computer crime. Although the police produce crime statistics, the fact that computer crime is not a legal term means that there are no police-produced computer crime statistics for Scotland.

Nevertheless, there are a number of reliable sources throughout the UK and abroad, that indicate the extent of computer security in general. Typical sources include the Audit Commission, the dti, and the Computer Security Institute. The aforementioned CSI 2000 Survey, actually highlights a decrease in computer crime. Examples of decreases include: Web vandalism (down from 98 incidents in 1999, to 64 incidents in 2000); Financial Fraud (27, 3); Denial of Service attacks (93, 60); and Theft of Transaction Information (25, 8).

This is not to be complacent. Although Business-to-Business transactions on the Web are now well established, there is a slow take-up of Business-to-Consumer transactions, the latter the result of customer fears over security (Aubrey-Jones [5]). The public perception, via media publicity, is playing a large part in the growth, or lack of it, in Business-to-Customer transactions. Previously, if a company suffered graffiti on its physical buildings, the impact to the public and the organization was minimal; but, place the same graffiti on a company's Website, and the impact can be immediate: Web business can be suspended to fix the security vulnerability and customer confidence on the organisation's ability to protect customer data suddenly becomes an issue. The result can be loss of business.

According to a report by the International Chamber of Commerce's Commercial Crime Services unit [6], 2,776 of the 4,139 cases referred to the chamber by its members were directly connected to crime, fraud or deliberate misrepresentation by website traders offering bogus goods or services. It is clear that computer crime, particularly with the advent of E-Business, is here to stay. That is not to adopt a defeatist attitude but, instead, an effort at facing reality so as to be better placed to tackle computer crime.

Although there are many stakeholders in the field of computer security (Biggam and Hogarth [7]) – business community, police, hardware/software vendors, researchers, etc. - the purpose of this paper is to look at the role of universities in contributing towards the field of computer security and to show, specifically, how Soft Systems Methodology could be used to assist in the development of a computer security teaching module.

2.   TACKLING COMPUTER SECURITY: A UNIVERSITY PERSPECTIVE

How can an organization tackle computer security? It is a simple matter to say that an organization ought to implement a standard such as BS7799, or hire consultants to implement a Firewall, but a key issue is how an organization can determine its initial security requirements (Biggam and Hogarth [8]).

There are many stakeholders involved in the field of computer security, including:
- Business community
- Police
- Perpetrator(s)
- Hardware/software vendors
- Researchers
- Users

Each of these stakeholders have different roles to play, but one stakeholder that ought to play a more active role, is the University. Universities often contribute in terms of important research (notable examples include London School of Economics and Leicester University), but it is in the teaching of computer security that universities ought to play a more active role.

Within Scotland, there are 13 universities:
1. University of Glasgow
2. University of Strathclyde
3. Glasgow Caledonian University
4. University of Paisley
5. University of Stirling
6. University of Edinburgh
7. Heriot-Watt University
8. Napier University
9. University of Dundee
10. Abertay University

11. University of Aberdeen
12. Robert Gordon University
13. St Andrew's University

In terms of teaching computer security, all of the above universities have some element of computer security within their teaching syllabus. However, it is interesting to note the context in which computer security is taught. All the universities teach computer security from a technical perspective, and so it is no surprise to see the subject taught within computer science, or equivalent, departments. Even then, though, computer security is not taught as a module in its own right, but rather as aspects of other modules (e.g. Systems Development, Computer Programming, etc.). There is a reasonable case that security ought to be integrated with other computing subjects (because business when they develop their computer systems, ought to integrate their security with their systems development process), but, equally, in terms of student learning, computer subjects are often separated (Computer Organization, Networks, Programming, Web Design, etc.).

It is also surprising not to find evidence of a computer security module within business-type departments in Scotland. The business community regularly suffers from security breaches, and so it makes sense to educate those who will work in that community to aid in the security of that environment. Although technical solutions to security problems are valued, it is the business case that determines whether or not security is treated seriously within an organization.

One of the universities – Glasgow Caledonian University (GCU) – attempted to address the issue of incorporating a computer security module within its School of Business. The following sections describe how GCU used the Soft Systems Methodology (SSM) to facilitate this development.

3.   CAPTURING SECURITY REQUIREMENTS USING SSM

What is SSM and why is it suited to capturing computer security requirements? SSM was developed in the 1980s by Checkland [9] and Checkland and Scholes [10] to "enhance problem situations". Where the system issues were clear-cut and well-defined, then the solution could be derived through a technical methodology, such as SSADM (Ashworth and Goodland [11]). Where the system issues were unclear or fuzzy, then SSM was recommended as a means of clarifying the problems. In other words,

SSM was not intended primarily as a means of producing technical solutions, but rather as a vehicle to facilitate the clarification of (softer) issues.

A simple perspective is to view system methodologies within two opposing camps: hard methodologies (such as SSADM) with their emphasis on technical solutions and soft methodologies (such as SSM) with their emphasis on people/organizational issues. However the reality is complicated, with methodologies ranging in various degrees between 'hard' and 'soft': Mumfords and Land's socio-technical approach, RAD, DSDM, JAD, etc. (Avison and Fitzgerald [12]; Hogarth and Biggam [13]).

SSM is a useful way to capture user requirements. SSM concentrates on stakeholder perspectives and thus facilitates user involvement. In addition, the tools used (CATWOE and Rich Pictures) are easy to employ and understand: this allows continued participation of user groups. The major benefit of SSM is the desire to move from "the problem unstructured" to "the problem structured" to "desirable changes".

This approach to systems analysis is well-suited to security issues: too often the technical solution is assumed (e.g. Firewall) without much thought given to user requirements or stakeholder perspectives. SSM would allow organizations to understand their security issues, clarify their security needs (including technical requirements) and so be better placed to protect their assets. It is interesting to note that ICL, through the use of their Business Impact Assessment methodology, adopt a 'soft' approach to ascertaining an organization's security requirements.

Users are an important group of stakeholders who have a critical role in the capture of user requirements. It ought to be emphasized that their value in the systems development process, particularly in the capture of user requirements, is not only recognized by Checkland but by researchers in other fields, e.g. computer security (Adams and Sasses [14]; Rannenberg [15]).

4.   USING SSM TO ASCERTAIN TEACHING MODULE REQUIREMENTS: GLASGOW CALEDONIAN UNIVERSITY (GCU)

The following example illustrates how SSM could be used to capture user requirements. When the Division of Business Information Management (BIM) at GCU was interested in developing a computer security module for undergraduate students, SSM was used to clarify module requirements. The choice of SSM was based on two reasons: one, module issues were initially ill-defined; and two, SSM was known to the module leader, and so the exercise in using SSM, initially, was borne out of curiosity.

SSM has gone through various changes since its inception, but the SSM structure adopted for this exercise was:

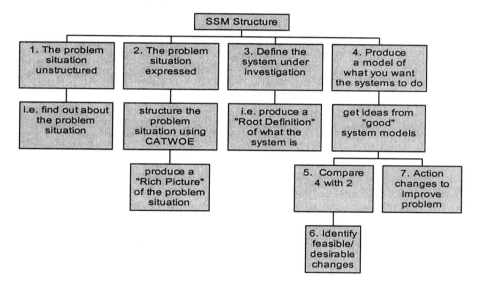

Figure 2. SSM Structure

4.1   Stage 1: The Problem Situation Unstructured

There was a desire for additional undergraduate modules at undergraduate levels 3 and 4 (ordinary and honours, respectively) within the School of Business in general, and within the Division of Business Information Management (BIM) in particular. At the same time, a number of staff, with previous experience of teaching computer security within a different department, but now residing in BIM, expressed an interest in developing a teaching module in computer security. Although BIM had taught some aspects of computer security to undergraduate students (e.g. backup procedures, the need for password control, etc), the delivery of a full module devoted to security was something new. As such, the initial module requirements were unclear and fuzzy.

Problem situation unstructured:

Figure 3. Rich Picture Element

4.2   Stage 2: The problem Situation Expressed

Two tools that are used in SSM to "enhance the problem situation" are CATWOE and Rich Pictures. Each aids in clarifying roles and issues. In the context of module development, the use of CATWOE resulted in the following listing:

C   Customers (i.e. beneficiaries of the 'system' i.e. module):
     Students; BIM, School of Business; Business Community; Staff (in terms of staff development)
A   Actors (i.e. those who carry out essential activities in the module):
     Module team; BIM (supplying resources); School of Business (in terms of validation and quality control); externals (academic and business); students (lectures/seminars/labs/assessments/feedback)
T   Transaction (i.e. change expected to take place):
     Module idea – Module delivery
W   Weltanschauung (i.e. stakeholder perspectives): See Rich Picture
O   Owners (i.e. person/group to whom module team are responsible):
     BIM (Subject Quality Group); School of Business
E   Environment (i.e. environment in which relevant system is placed):
     Module resides in BIM, but offered to all Business students

The use of CATWOE helped identify the main stakeholders together with the target audience.

4.3   Stage 2: The Rich Picture

The Rich Picture produced was essentially a cartoon illustrating issues to be tackled to produce a successful module in computer security. This picture helped visualize a complex mess of interacting people, roles, threats, facts, observations, etc. Some of the elements of this Rich Picture are shown below:

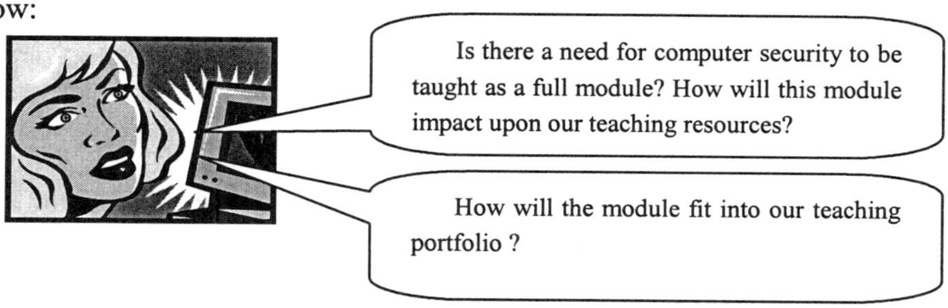

Is there a need for computer security to be taught as a full module? How will this module impact upon our teaching resources?

How will the module fit into our teaching portfolio ?

Figure 4. BIM Rich Picture Element Expressing Staff Views

How does this module fit into our degree portfolio ?
Are there any prerequisites?
How does it help us to get a job?
What are the assessment requirements?

Figure 5. STUDENTS Rich Picture Element Expressing Student Views

The Rich Picture highlighted a number of issues, including:
- Rationale for a module in computer security
- Module content
- Resourcing (staff, supporting research, hardware, software, rooms)
- Student interests
- External support (academic and business)

Although there are existing module development processes used within BIM to facilitate module development and validation, the use of SSM assisted the module leader in clarifying module issues in a simple and straightforward manner. The use of Rich Pictures was particularly beneficial in visualizing non-technical issues.

4.4   Stage 3: Define the System under Investigation

Initially, this stage was viewed as less helpful than the previous stages. The 'system' as such was a teaching module, which, within the University environment, was clearly understood. However, what did materialize was the need to fit the module content within the context of a business environment, to reflect the principal teaching theme within BIM. Thus, "Computer Security" as a title was replaced with the title "Business Information Systems Security".

4.5   Stage 4: Produce a Model of what you want the System to do.

This stage was interpreted as developing the actual module descriptor at an appropriate level for undergraduate students. The Learning Outcomes reflected industry concerns:

- Security Trends
- Security Life Cycle
- Risk Assessment
- Security approaches and standards (e.g. BS7799)
- Disaster Recovery
- Legal Issues (e.g. Computer Misuse Act 1990; Data Protection Act 1998)
- E-Business Security (e.g. PKI)
- Ethics
- Miscellaneous (e.g. Computer Forensics, Biometrics)

4.6   Stage 5: Compare Proposed Model (in Stage 4) with Rich Picture (in Stage 2) to determine if Problem Situation is Resolved

A number of problems were identified. Stage 2 highlighted the need for a module to meet the needs of business students, but the initial module descriptor was found to be too technical in nature, thus seen as inappropriate to business students. The module descriptor was then changed (but not in terms of subject headings) to reflect the subject content and target audience.

The assessment process was another key issue that was highlighted. The Rich Picture revealed one aspect of University thought, that new modules ought to consider new modes of module delivery and assessment:

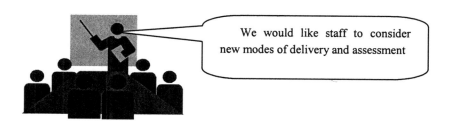

Figure 6. UNIVERSITY Rich Picture Element Expressing University View

The module descriptor developed at stage 4 had not taken this on board. The traditional approach to teaching revolved around the lectures/labs/seminar model, and assessment was normally weighted towards end-of-semester examinations. The staff involved in the module delivery were concerned about making radical changes to the traditional teaching model and so retained the lecture format but made the seminars and labs student-centred. In terms of the assessment, it was decided to get the students to produce a mock conference paper (including abstract, etc.) for the coursework and to alter the traditional weighting between coursework and exam: 70% coursework (conference paper), 30% class test.

4.7   Stages 6 and 7: Identify Feasible Changes and Action Changes

The module was successfully validated and implemented in academic year 1999-2000, Semester B, to honours students in the School of Business. Student feedback, via standard university questionnaires, was overwhelmingly positive. The academic external praised the assessment. One criticism highlighted the need for software illustrating BS7799. This deficiency was corrected for the next academic year.

5.   CONCLUSION

Computer security is a field worthy of academic study, not only in terms of research but within the context of teaching. However, there are difficulties introducing computer security in to the university curriculum as a subject in its own right:

- Who owns the module?

- How does it fit into the School/Faculty/Department/Division portfolio?
- Do the resources exist particularly with respect to staff expertise and research?
- Who is the target audience?
- What level ought it be aimed?
- and what should be the module content?

Using SSM is a simple and practical way to clarify some of these issues. Particularly useful is the easy-to-use tools CATWOE and Rich Pictures. An additional benefit of SSM, not initially realized in the case study, was that a straight-forward record of development was recorded, mostly of a visual nature (i.e. Rich Pictures), allowing a quick appreciation of the issues that were raised and tackled from inception to fruition.

Although SSM was used in this paper to facilitate the development of a computer security module appropriate to undergraduate students, the use of SSM is not restricted to module development. Perhaps organizations ought to consider using SSM as a front-end means of clarifying their security requirements.

6.   REFERENCES

[1] Biggam, J. (2001). 'Defining Knowledge: an Epistemological foundation for Knowledge Management", *Proceedings of the Thirty-Fourth Annual Hawaii International Conference on System Sciences*, IEEE, January 2001.
[2] Gollmann, D. (2000). *Computer Security*, John Wiley & Sons, Cambridge.
[3] Martin, B. (2001). 'Attrition' Web site: Http://www.attrition.org/security
[4] Computer Security Institute (2000). 'Computer Security issues & Trends', CSI/FBI Survey, Vol VI No. 1, Spring 2000
[5] Aubrey-Jones, D. (1999). 'Web Browser Security', *Proceedings of The 16th World Conference on Computer Security, Audit & Control*, Elsevier Advanced Technology.
[6] Commercial Crime Services (2000). *Report on Computer Fraud*, International Chamber of Commerce, London.
[7] Biggam, J. and Hogarth, A. (2000). 'Information Systems Security in the Age of Electronic Commerce', *Conference Proceedings of Management Information Systems 2000*, Lisbon, June.
[8] Biggam, J. and Hogarth, A. (1996). The Development of a 'Computer Security Requirement Specification': Embedding and Merging ICL's 'Business Impact Model' with Soft Systems Methodology (SSM), *Proceedings of the 3rd BCS Information Systems Methodologies Specialist Group Conference, University College Cork*, Eire.
[9] Checkland, P. B. (1981). *Systems Thinking: Systems Practice*. Wiley, Chichester.
[10]   Checkland, P. B. and Scholes, J. (1991). *Soft Systems Methodology in Action*. Wiley, Chichester.

[11]   Ashworth, C. and Goodland, M. (1990). *SSADM A Practical Approach*. McGraw-Hill International Series in Software Engineering, London.

[12]   Avison, D. E. and Fitzgerald, G. (1992). *Information Systems Development Methodologies, techniques and Tools*. Blackwell Scientific Publishing, Oxford.

[13]   Hogarth, A. and Biggam, J. (2000). 'The Social and Technical Effects of Introducing Groupware into the Educational Environment', *Proceedings of The ACM/OCG Conference on Educational Information and Communication Technology (EDICT 2000)*, Vienna.

[14]   Adams, A. and Sasse, M. A. (1999). 'Users are not the enemy: why users compromise security mechanisms and how to take remedial measures', *Communications of the ACM*, 42(12), pp.40-46.

[15]   Rannenberg, K. (2000). 'Multilateral security – a concept and examples for balanced security', *Proceedings of the 9th ACM New Security Paradigms Workshop 2000*, September, Cork, Ireland, ACM Press.

1.   INTRODUCTION

The advent of BS7799, which has been adopted by countries like AS 4444 in Australia and has been accepted as an ISO 17799 standard, was hailed as a major advance in security management, but having given seminars on Information Security Management Standards to security officers, one gains the impression that the gap between theory and practice is still very wide.

In fact one is sometimes left with the suspicion that the Standards may have done more to solve the problems of security audit and training organizations, than those of the security officer. Of course, the security officer can take out insurance and persuade management to fund a compliance audit. The results of such an audit will enable the security officer to either:

- Display a certificate on the wall, or

- Present management with a list of resources necessary to acquire such a certificate.

But then what? How does the security officer set about ensuring that the organization, which will probably have an ever increasing business dependency on its expanding and vulnerable I.T. system, is as well protected as limited security resources allow?

A security incident could cause serious financial losses to an organization, its partners and clients. In these litigious days the security officer could well face a hostile barrister, in the aftermath of such a security incident. It is not difficult to predict the type of questions that would be asked; formulating convincing responses might be more problematic. How can security officers demonstrate that they take all reasonable efforts, to optimally deploy security resources?

Accountants have long since recognized that their professional competence may be demonstrated by a pristine set of financial records. An accountant will probably give a high priority to the maintenance of such records, when accepting a new appointment. Hence accountancy students are taught bookkeeping in their first year, however, few information security courses and textbooks provide an insight in the development and maintenance of information security documentation.

It is suggested that a comprehensive set of security documentation can serve to guide the security officer to an optimal information security stance, and to provide convincing evidence that a reasonable standard of professional competence had been maintained.

Security documentation can, inter alias:

- Document all significant policies pertinent to information security;

- Provide details of all systems and environments for which the officer has security responsibilities;

- Specify the security officer's responsibilities as formulated by senior management;

- Specify the degree to which some of those responsibilities have been delegated;

- Document the security systems and procedures developed in response to those responsibilities;

- Provide clear pointers to security logs and records, and reporting/ archiving responsibilities;

- Record the outcomes and subsequent actions, following risk analysis and security audits;

- Facilitate the design of security systems for new and enhanced IT systems;

- Facilitate audit and compliance exercises; and

- Provide senior management with an overview of the organization's security stance.

It is therefore suggested that the security officer should give careful consideration to the development and continual maintenance of an appropriate set of security documentation. Having said that leads to the obvious follow up question - how?

The standards such as BS7799 group together security topics, and implicitly encourage a top down approach to security management, but they do not explicitly advise the security manager on the development of security documentation. Indeed, one of the significant dangers of the standards is that they will encourage the formation of security documentation, which serves to facilitate compliance audits, but does little to enhance organizational I.T. security.

In this paper the role of security documentation is discussed and some suggestions are provided on the development of electronic documentation to facilitate information security management.

2.   TOTAL SET OF SECURITY DOCUMENTATION

2.1   Overview

The potential applications of information security documentation were listed above and this list provides an insight into the proposed set of documentation. Since we are dealing with information security in a complex and dynamic I.T. environment, the documentation should clearly be maintained in electronic form, with databases employed for all items comprising significant amounts of detail, and html linkages between relevant sections.

The proposed sections of the security documentation are:

- Policies,

- Information Assets,

- Systems and Environments,

- Responsibilities,

- Security Systems and Procedures,

- Records, Reporting and Archiving,

- Security Audits and Business Continuity Planning,

- System Development, and

- Compliance.

The various proposed sections are described in outline below.

2.2   Policies

Organizational security policies commonly come in one of three varieties - the *non-existent*, the *bland* and the *treatise on passwords*. The security officer is well advised to explore and document all the implicit and explicit organizational policies, which could have some impact upon information security. These policies may then be used to establish the various aspects of the organization's information security policy.

Organizations will have, at least implicit, policies to ensure their continued existence, by abiding with all legislative, regulatory and contractual requirements. Such requirements commonly have implications for the integrity, availability and often confidentiality, of certain records and hence on security requirements.

The assets and finances of an organization are subject to control and recording policies: authorizations, four eyes principles, segregation of duties, audit trails etc. As such manual processes migrate to I.T. systems, these policies also remain as significant security requirements.

Some policy areas may have more subtle impacts upon information security. The deleterious effects of offensive email, in a climate increasing sensitivity to harassment and discrimination issues, were easily predicted. Nevertheless some organizations still lack systems and procedures to respond to such misuse of information systems. Similarly social concerns may lead to demands for accessibility to certain organizational information, or for dial up access for classes of disadvantaged employees, with attendant network security implications.

The part of Privacy Policy that related to the protection of personal data will clearly have implications to information security. The current and emerging laws on intellectual property will also be a major concern, particularly in terms of installed software and material downloaded from the Web.

Personnel policies, and related outsourcing issues, will have less subtle impacts upon information security, particularly if they produce a high level of mobility amongst privileged information system users, or contract out I.T. processing without strict contractual requirements on information security.

The information security officer would thus be well advised to hold documentation on all relevant management policies, to consider them and to report upon their implications for the organizational security policy.

2.3   Information Assets

The security officer is responsible for the protection of the information assets, but what are these assets and what degrees of priority are given to them? The problem of assigning dollar values to electronic files was recognized in the days of Courtney Risk Analysis [1], and the current problem is much more complex than that. The questions faced by the security officer are, inter alias, *what is the business impact arising from the:*

- Loss of confidentiality of this data item

- Loss of integrity of this data item;

- Unauthorized invocation of this transaction; and

- Loss of availability of this business process for this specified period of time.

Even the development of an inventory of the total set of data assets is a task ranging from the mammoth to the impossible. Nevertheless the security officer should at least document classes of data and business processes, together with a mapping to the systems storing, processing and transmitting those classes, and if possible an impact rating of the classes. Given the draconian laws arising on intellectual property the security officer will need to maintain a register of all installed software and license agreements.

2.4   Systems and Environments

It is self evident that the security officer should document the relevant details of all IT systems, buildings etc. within their aegis. The problem is to ensure that this documentation is continually updated in current networked environments. Ideally the I.T. departments would supply this information electronically, and security officers then merely require a linkage from this documentation. In such a case, is there some mechanism by which the security officer can highlight recent actual or proposed changes so that the security implications can be considered?

At the other end of the spectrum, the production and maintenance of this aspect of the documentation may be extremely time consuming. Such a situation is one requiring urgent attention, since it implies that the security officers are not adequately informed of the systems and environments they are required to protect.

2.5   Responsibilities

No security system is 100% effective and security officers commonly complain of a lack of support from senior management. In these circumstances security officers cannot guarantee that security incidents never arise, and they will implicitly bear some degree of responsibility for any consequent business impacts. Hence the security officers would be wise to obtain a full statement of their own responsibilities, and develop an organizational chart showing the explicit delegation of those responsibilities.

The security officer should also be in a position to call upon a full description of the security responsibilities of all employees, contractors etc. In the event of a security incident this documentation should be able to highlight either:

- The individuals that failed to meet their security responsibilities, or

- Inadequate, or unrealistic, specification of security responsibilities.

Delegation of security responsibilities also implies a commitment to ensure that such delegations are not unreasonable in terms of the expectations placed upon employees. Hence this set of documentation should also contain full details of the proposed and actual systems for security training, with links to training material, course details, staff attendances etc.

2.6   Security Systems and Procedures

The documentation must clearly contain details of security systems, e.g. firewalls, VPNs, swipe card access control, virus protection software, authentication servers etc. and associated procedures, e.g. allocation of access privileges and passwords. Much of this material is commonly embedded in other documentation and, in the first instance, a comprehensive set of linkages should be established.

The security officer clearly needs to have access to such details of security systems and procedures in the first instance. However, this section of the documentation also provides an insight into the role of the security officer, because it raises a number of significant questions:

- How do these security systems and procedures correlate with the *systems and environments* documentation (See 2.4)?

- What are the role of these security systems and procedures, i.e. what assets are they protecting against what threats?

- What are the threats and assets that are not covered by these systems and procedures?

- Are the strongest security systems and procedures directed to the highest areas of risk?

- What is the degree of effectiveness of the systems and procedures - prioritised in order of risk?

- Do any of these systems and procedures represent, in themselves, single points of failure?

- Are these systems and procedures themselves vulnerable to attack?

Clearly these questions cannot be answered by an inventory of security systems and procedures. Such a discussion involves the complex linkages between all the entities involved in a risk analysis: threats, systems (physical and logical), vulnerabilities, security systems, information assets and the organizational reliance upon those assets. The security officer requires an effective active security model to tackle these questions (See 3). A security officer would do well to reflect that the questions posed above could well be asked by a hostile barrister, in legal case following security incident that caused financial loss to other parties.

2.7   Records, Reporting and Archiving

Senior management, legal and law enforcement advice is essential, to develop a full understanding of the security officer's responsibilities in protecting and/or maintaining:

- Organizational reports and archives as required by senior management policy, regulatory or legislative bodies; and

- Operating and security logs and reports.

This section of the security documentation should contain details of those sets of data, e.g. tax return information, essential to ensure organizational compliance with contractual, legal, regulatory or legislative requirements.

Linkages or cross references to other sections of the security documentation are also recommended e.g.

- Systems and environments (See 2.4): where are the records stored and processed?

- Responsibilities (See 2.5): who are responsible for their security?

- Security systems and procedures (See 2.6): what are the security provisions for their protection?

- Security audits (See 2.8): were any recommendations made for their protection and what subsequent action was taken?

The operating and security logs and reports are clearly of vital importance. This set of documentation should be headed by all relevant advice, from legal and law enforcement agencies, on the collection, handling and retention of such data, particularly in respect of data that may be used in legal proceedings.

In addition to the security reports and logs themselves, this section must contain all relevant supporting documentation to ensure that the reports and logs can at some later date be fully exploited in investigations and, if necessary, submitted in legal proceedings. Linkages and cross references to other documentation will include, inter alias:

- Systems and environments (See 2.4) to ensure that details as of the date that the records were taken are available; and

- Responsibilities (See 2.5) particularly in relation to capturing security data.

2.8   Security Audits and Business Continuity Planning

A comprehensive set of security documentation will greatly facilitate security audits, and security audit reports etc. can themselves be a valuable component of security documentation. Such reports will normally provide an overview of the security situation at the time of the audit and a series of recommendations.

The security officer should document not only the reports but also the follow up actions to the recommendations; including a follow- up schedule, showing the progress of implementation and also reasons for delayed or non-implementation. There is ample material available on the documentation of Business Continuity Planning and it is suggested that such documentation may also be maintained in this section, with appropriate linkages to the other sections.

2.9 System Development

In many cases security officers have responsibility for protecting systems that were not designed with a high priority given to security. Hence it is important that a security officer provides well-documented and reasoned cases for security implementation in new or upgraded systems. In the cases of system modification or upgrade the security officer needs to give careful consideration to:

- The risks of the current system;

- The security, and security rationale, provided against those risks;

- The risks of the proposed system;

- Proposed removal of any erstwhile security systems or procedures; and

- The security and security rationale to be provided against the risks of the proposed system.

If the risks, security and security rationale of the erstwhile system were adequately documented then this exercise is greatly facilitated. If such documentation is not available then there is a significant danger that system changes will introduce new risks, or remove undocumented, but important, security systems or procedures of the original system. The discussion in a proposed security model (See 3) is relevant to this section.

2.10 Compliance

This section of the documentation should provide an overview of the security stance of the organization and highlight any major areas of concern by cross linkages, e.g. management policies that are not being met by current security systems and practices, security audit recommendations still outstanding, inadequate security logging in case of a security incident etc.

In this section the security officer would be wise to make a detailed list of security recommendations for senior management, and record them for that interview with the hostile barrister.

3.   SECURITY MODEL

3.1   Overview

One of the major problems with most security documentation is that it is commonly embedded in documentation intended for another purpose, e.g. Operating Manuals, System Design Reports etc. Documentation intended primarily for security purposes tends to be addressed at a macro level, e.g. standards, risk analysis report. Information at this level tends to focus on *what security is to be achieved* rather than how *to achieve it.* Rarely does one read current documentation and feel that it gives a genuine insight into the security stance of an organizational system, i.e. it is often difficult to answer the major questions of the security officer: where do I need to focus attention, what are the priorities for the future.

The Risk Data Repository (RDR) [2-4] was developed some years ago as a risk analysis model, and during this work it became clear that the RDR also provided an insight into the requirements for security documentation. A prototype system was developed in Visual Basic and current work is directed to developments, which could make more effective use of PC browsers to handle the linkages amongst the entities. It also clear that the early RDR did not adequately address the role of networks.

Nevertheless the RDR described entities in terms of their roles from a security viewpoint, demonstrated the security inter-relationships of those entities and facilitated the computation of risk parameters. The entities of the earlier model are being replaced with a greater emphasis on networks and countermeasures. It is suggested that this model provides a basis for security documentation in electronic form that can:

- Be easily updated in rapidly evolving environments; and

- Facilitate the extraction of security information for various purposes, e.g. risk analysis, security design etc.

3.2   Structure of Security Entities

In the discussion on documentation above it was suggested that the security officer maintain documentation on *Information Assets, Systems and*

Environments, Security Systems and Procedures and *System Development*. It was also noted that it would normally be quite difficult to extract the information required by the security officer from current documentation.

It is suggested that a security model could provide a means by which a security officer records the relevant security information and gradually builds up application packages to assist in the analysis of that information. In the first instance the entities of the model are defined, followed by the security linkages for such entities. The proposed entities relate the physical and logical aspects of security. At the top end of the model the *Information Assets* are processed by *Application Systems*, which in turn are hosted by *Virtual Networks*. These *Virtual Networks* are in turn hosted by *Physical Networks*. The *Physical Networks* comprise a set of interconnected *Units*, and are located in *Physical Platforms*, which themselves are located in a *Physical Environment*.

The purpose of the model is to highlight the security inter-relationships between the entities in a manner that facilitates the task of the security officer. The major entities included in the model are:

- A Unit - individual item of equipment + plus its accessories. Unit come in four categories End User (EU), Server (SU), Sensitive Data Storage Unit (SDSU) and Coms (CU) (NB cabling and wireless is considered as a Coms Unit).

- A PHYSICAL NETWORK (PN) - a collection of interconnected Units, one or more of which is a cabling or wireless Unit.

- A PHYSICAL PLATFORM (PP) - a collection of standalone Units and all SDSUs and physical networks located in a physical area.

- A PHYSICAL ENVIRONMENT - a collection of sites and buildings with associated essential services and physical security functions that hosts Physical Platforms.

- A VIRTUAL NETWORK (VN) - one or more physical networks, with common security architecture and / or a grouping associated with an AS.

- AN APPLICATION SYSTEM (AS) - one or more virtual networks used to host an information processing and/or communication application.

- INFORMATION ASSETS (IA) - data and processes, which, if attacked, could cause significant harm to the organization.

- INTRINSIC THREATS (IT) - those events that may cause harm to information assets and whose occurrence cannot be prevented, e.g. environmental threats (fire, extreme weather conditions), personnel physical (damage or misuse of equipment) and personnel logical (attacks mounted over networks etc).

These entities have, however, been chosen so that the linkages between them provide security officers with an insight into the security of their systems. These linkages are described in the next section.

3.3   Inter-relationships of Security Entities

The security entities described in the previous section are inter-related from a security viewpoint. The emphasis is now on the physical network, as the logical grouping of equipment items. If a building (Physical Environment) hosting a Physical Platform is damaged by some intrinsic threat event, e.g. fire, the security officer will be more interested in the effect upon a Physical Network than an individual item of equipment. Any standalone items will be separately linked to the Physical Platform and to the Application System. The security entities facilitate the tracing of threat events to their ultimate consequence, which is a business impact. If the model is recorded as an electronic document, with html links, then the security officer can easily postulate a number of potential intrinsic threats and then trace their likely paths to determine the ultimate business impact. The threats may be classified as:

- Environmental (e.g. flooding): impacting upon Physical Environments,

- Personnel Physical (e.g. attacker enters secure area containing an SDSU): impacting upon Physical Platforms, and

- Personnel Logical (e.g. attacker gaining access to sensitive server over a network): impacting upon Virtual Networks.

Having traced an attack the security officer will then be concerned with the degree to which the security measures mitigate such an attack. In this model it is suggested that such security measures can be effectively represented as Threat Countermeasure Diagrams [5]. In this approach each countermeasure is considered to counter the incident threat but also to introduce consequent threats arising from loopholes in the countermeasure or attacks on the countermeasure itself. Supporting countermeasures are commonly employed to address these consequent threats, and a Threat Countermeasure Diagram is an effective means of representing such countermeasure rationale.

4.   CONCLUSIONS

The life of an airline pilot is sometimes described as hours of boredom followed by minutes of sheer terror. The life of a security officer could similarly be described as years of frustration, followed by weeks of severe recrimination. Effective security documentation can be a means by which security officers can:

- Gain an enhanced awareness of their roles and the procedures to fulfil those roles;

- Provide evidence to senior management on necessary security systems and procedures; and

- Provide evidence on their professional competence.

It has also been suggested in this paper that such documentation could be significantly enhanced by an electronic security based similar to the Risk Data Repository described in previous papers.

5.   REFERENCES

[1]   Courtney, R.H. JR., "Security risk assessment in electronic data processing systems." *AFIPS Conference Proceedings 1977*, pp.97-104.

[2]   Anderson, A.M., Longley, D., and Tickle, A.B., "The Risk Data Repository: A Novel Approach to Security Risk Modelling". *Computer Security, Proc. IFIP TC 11 9th Int. Conf. on Information Security* (Editor Dougall), IFIP Sec.'93, Toronto, Canada, 12-14 May 1993, NY:Elsevier Science Publishers, 1993, 185-190.

[3]   Anderson A, Kwok L F and Longley D, "Security Modelling for Organisations", *Proc. of 2nd ACM Conf on Computer and Communication Security*, Fairfax Virginia, USA, 2-4 Nov 1994, pp.241-250.

[4]   Kwok L F and Longley D, "A Security Officers' Workbench", *Computers and Security*, Vol.15, No. 8, 1996, 695-705.

[5]   Caelli, W., Longley, D., and Tickle, A.B. "A Methodology for Describing Information and Physical Security Architectures". *IT Security: The Need for International Cooperation, Proc. IFIP TC11 8th Int. Conf. on Information Security* (Editors Gable and Caelli), IFIP Sec.'92, Singapore, 27-29 May 1992, NY:Elsevier Science Publishers, 1992, 277-296.

TRANSACTION BASED RISK ANALYSIS - USING COGNITIVE FUZZY TECHNIQUES

ELME SMITH[1], JAN H.P. ELOFF[2]
[1] smithe@unisa.ac.za.
University of South Africa, Department of Computer Science and Information Systems, PO Box 392, PRETORIA 0003, Republic of South Africa
Tel: (+2712) 429-6309
Fax: (+2712) 429-6848
[2] eloff@rkw.rau.ac.za.
Rand Afrikaans University, Department of Computer Science, PO Box 524, AUCKLAND PARK 2006, Republic of South Africa
Tel: (+2711) 489-2842
Fax: (+2711) 489-2138

Key words: cognitive fuzzy-logic approach; fuzzy cognitive map; information security; risk analysis; risk assessment; risk-management methodology; transactions

Abstract: This paper is devoted to the presentation of a risk-management methodology specifically developed for assessing and analysing risks incurred by the business transactions of an organisation. A transaction is a part of a business information system that has one or other functional goal. An order-entry-and-delivering-of-goods transaction forming part of an MRP (materials, requirement & planning) information system is discussed as an example. The proposed methodology includes five successive stages in all, namely initiation, domain analysis, risk assessment, risk analysis and domain monitoring. This paper focuses on the risk analysis stage.

The methodology enhances risk management in that it incorporates cognitive fuzzy-logic techniques – as opposed to quantitative techniques such as annual loss exposure (ALE) calculation – to assess and analyse the risks. In this way, it is ensured that full cognisance is taken of the intuitive nature of human observation when assessing and analysing the possible risks to be incurred in an organisation. In addition, the methodology takes into account the vagueness of the decision making process with respect to securing transaction information.

1.   INTRODUCTION

Information technology is currently being employed in business environments across the globe, resulting in significant improvements in the efficiency and quality of all services rendered. The occurrence of a risk, such as the exposure of highly confidential and sensitive transaction data to outsiders, could compromise not only the customer's privacy, but also quite literally the well-being of the organisation. It is, imperative, therefore, to be able to identify possible risks in good time and to implement the necessary security controls in order to protect the business as a whole.

Broadly speaking, risk management can be defined as that process by means of which security controls are identified and implemented that will, at best, prevent risks from occurring and, at worst, minimise their effect if they were to occur [1-3]. In currently available risk-management techniques the emphasis has, however, mainly been placed on the input and manipulation of numbers. Human common sense and intuition, which form the basis of any risk-management exercise, are most of the time neglected. These techniques, furthermore, address risk analysis from an information- and resources-asset point of view. They require organisations to identify all assets, followed by the identification of the applicable risks. Risks identified in such a way are not modelled from a business point of view. Management might be interested to know what risks are involved during the execution of a specific type of business transaction. It is, therefore, essential to protect the transaction as a basic business unit.

The principal aim of this paper is, therefore, not to discourage the use of powerful risk-management techniques (such as CRAMM), but rather to propose a new way of handling risk management in an integrated business environment. The methodology incorporates both the vague and intuitive aspects of the normal business environment by following a cognitive fuzzy-logic approach to the assessment and analysis of risks that might be incurred in this environment. The methodology is aimed at identifying the high-risk areas within a typical business environment. The methodology also helps to manage risks by facilitating the decision-making process with respect to securing information assets.

The proposed methodology includes five successive stages in all, namely initiation, domain analysis, risk assessment, risk analysis and domain monitoring. The first section of the paper will be devoted to a synoptic and high-level overview of the proposed methodology, followed by an in-depth discussion on the risk analysis stage.

2.   A HIGH-LEVEL OVERVIEW OF THE PROPOSED RISK-MANAGEMENT METHODOLOGY

The proposed risk-management methodology enhances risk management by considering the route that a business transaction follows within an organisation. Normally different sections within the organisation execute different tasks on the route that a transaction follows. Consider, for example, an *order-entry-and-delivering-of-goods transaction* in a retail environment. Such a transaction route can include different departments (sections) of the organisation, where each is responsible for a different task. Tasks forming part of such a transaction may include order entry, checking availability of stock, picking the stock and despatch the goods to the delivery address. A route that a transaction follows will further on be referred to as a *transaction information route*.

Transaction information routes indicate and identify all management processes and IT components that are required for the successful execution of a transaction. A transaction information route is used to assess and analyse the risks from an information security perspective. The advantage of performing risk analysis in this way is that composite risks from a business point of view can be calculated.

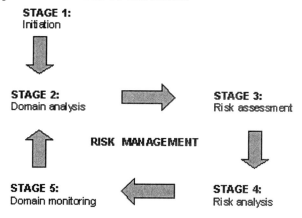

Figure 1. A graphic representation of the various stages in the proposed risk-management methodology

Information-technology risk management can be defined in terms of the proposed methodology as starting with an initiation stage (see figure 1). The methodology further includes four successive iterative stages, namely domain analysis, risk assessment, risk analysis and domain monitoring.

During the *first stage* (viz. initiation), the scope of the required risk-management project needs to be determined. The scope will on a high level identify the business transactions, also referred to as transaction information routes, that are of most importance to the organisation.

The identified transaction information routes will be analysed and disseminated in the *second stage* (viz. domain analysis). All the business sections participating during the execution of a transaction, identified during the previous phase, must be identified. A transaction information route comprises a fixed number of participating sections. A typical order-entry-and-delivery-of-goods transaction can, for example, include participation of the following business sections: order entry, checking availability of stock, picking the stock and despatching of goods.

Transaction information routes are further sub-divided into phases. A phase on a transaction information route represents the work done by a specific section. The technologies employed to store and process information during each phase of a transaction is vulnerable to risks. Different technologies (such as database files, paper files, microfilm and a LAN server) can be employed by each section during the execution of a transaction to store and process information. The model proposed in this paper promotes, or enforces, the different sections within an organisation to take responsibility for ownership of information assets. It is, therefore, essential that security controls be implemented in each phase at best to prevent or at least to minimise the risks that may possibly be incurred. The security controls already implemented must also be identified.

Figure 2 depicts a typical transaction information route for an *order-entry-and-delivering-of-goods* transaction in a retail environment.

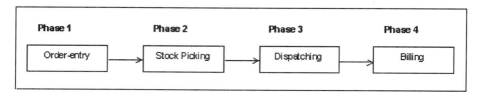

Figure 2. Route followed by an order-entry-and-delivering-of-goods transaction in a retail environment

The technologies and management processes employed in each phase to store and process transaction based information and the security controls implemented are not fixed, in the sense that the technologies and procedures can be upgraded and new security controls might be implemented over time. These technologies and procedures do not, however, exist in isolation. They interact and, in this way, exert a distinct influence on the possibility of risks incurring in an organisation. The more access capabilities and privileges defined for a transaction in a certain phase along a transaction information route, the greater the likelihood, for example, of the transaction's information being exposed to unauthorised parties. The risk management methodology proposed in this paper, therefore, considers not only the technologies and procedures that interact, but also their relationships with each other and their effect on the likelihood of IT risks being incurred.

The principal aim of the *third stage* (viz. risk-assessment) is to determine a risk value for *each phase* in a transaction information route. This risk value is based on the information-technology domain, including technology and management processes, of a transaction's information route. A cognitive fuzzy-modelling approach is followed to calculate risk values for each phase of a transaction information route. This approach ensures that full cognisance be taken of human common sense and intuition during the assessment and analysis of risks. As a detailed explanation of the cognitive fuzzy-modelling approach, for the risk assessment phase, falls outside the scope of this paper, the reader is referred to [4] for more information on this approach.

During the *fourth stage* (viz. risk analysis) decisions are made regarding the risk values calculated in the previous stage (that is, the risk-assessment stage). The risk-analysis stage is aimed at identifying high-risk transaction information routes (that is, *critical* transaction information routes) in a typical business environment with a view to enhancing the information security of such organization. The argumentation is that if management addresses the security problems exerted by the critical transaction information routes, the security issues in the less critical routes will also be addressed. This stage will be discussed in more detail in paragraph 3.

Finally, the organisation must be monitored during the *fifth stage* (viz. domain monitoring) in order to pinpoint any changes in its dynamic nature, including new risks that might occur. The latter stage, however, constitutes an ongoing process through which further or new risks could be identified that might even require a partial or complete iteration of the current risk-management methodology.

3.   STAGE 4: RISK ANALYSIS

The activities to be performed during the risk-analysis stage are depicted in figure 3.

3.1   Determine, which risk values, associated with each phase along a transaction information route give cause for concern. List the critical phases along each transaction information route (Stage 4 task 4.1)

During the risk-analysis stage, decisions are made regarding the risk values calculated for each phase along a specific transaction information route during the previous stage (that is, the risk-assessment stage). A phase could be classified as a "low-risk" phase if its risk value were to fall between 0 and 350, as a "medium-risk" phase if its risk value were to fall between 351 and 650 or as a "high-risk" phase, if its risk value were to fall between 651 and 1000. The latter classification is based on a numeric scale ranging from 0 to 1000, with 1000 representing the highest possible risk value. The phases classified as "high-risk" phases give cause for concern.

The risk-analysis stage is aimed at identifying high-risk transaction information routes (that is, *critical* transaction information routes) in an organization with a view to enhancing the information security of such organization.

STAGE 4: RISK ANALYSIS

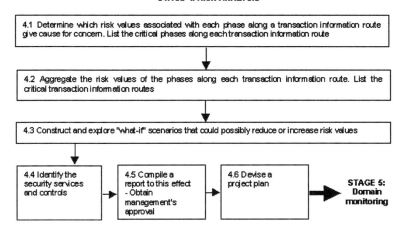

4.1 Determine which risk values associated with each phase along a transaction information route give cause for concern. List the critical phases along each transaction information route

4.2 Aggregate the risk values of the phases along each transaction information route. List the critical transaction information routes

4.3 Construct and explore "what-if" scenarios that could possibly reduce or increase risk values

| 4.4 Identify the security services and controls | 4.5 Compile a report to this effect - Obtain management's approval | 4.6 Devise a project plan | STAGE 5: Domain monitoring |

Figure 3. Stage 4: Risk Analysis

3.2 Aggregate the risk values of the phases along each transaction information route. List the critical transaction information routes (Stage 4 task 4.2)

The present methodology proposes a set of heuristics, summarised in table 1, for aggregating the risk values for all the phases along a specific transaction information route.

Table 1. Heuristics for aggregating risk values of a phase

Condition	Risk value of transaction route (R_{ROUTE})
Number of critical phases along transaction information route > 50%	$R_{ROUTE} = \sum_{i=1}^{m} R_i / m$, where m is the number of critical phases along the transaction information route and R_i is the risk value of the ith critical phase along the transaction information route.
Number of critical phases along transaction information route < 50%	$R_{ROUTE} = [\sum_{i=1}^{m} R_i + \sum_{j=1}^{n} R_j] / p$, where p is the number of phases along the transaction information route R_i is the risk value of the ith **critical** phase along the transaction information route R_j is the risk value of the jth **non-critical** phase along the transaction information route.

Number of critical phases along transaction information route > 50%	$R_{ROUTE} = \sum_{i=1}^{m} R_i / m$, where m is the number of critical phases along the transaction information route and R_i is the risk value of the ith critical phase along the transaction information route.

The aim of aggregating the risk values of all the phases along a specific transaction information route is to obtain an overall risk value for that transaction information route. Such risk value could then form the basis for identifying *critical transaction information routes* in the organisation. The classification of a transaction information route as a "high-risk", "medium-risk" or "low-risk" route is done in the same manner as that of the phases.

The complete set of transaction information routes in the organisation are analysed in a similar way. In this way, the high-risk areas in the organisation can be pinpointed. This will, in turn, present management with a clear picture of the specific transaction information routes to be followed in the organisation that need to be investigated when deciding on the implementation of security controls with a view to enhancing the information security of the organisation in question.

3.3   Construct and explore "what-if" scenarios that could possibly reduce or increase risk values (Stage 4 task 4.3)

The security related issues that play a vital role in the execution of the critical phases need to be identified and investigated. Examples of security related issues are the number of employees that are allowed access to the transaction information and the level of access rights allocated. The proposed methodology requires that the relationships between the various issues be established as they do not act in isolation, but interact with and influence each other. This will be discussed in more detail later on.

Security related issues occurring in an organisation are not easily quantified. Ideally, therefore, one wants a representation mechanism that can be used in a cognitive and intuitive manner to represent the relationships between these issues. A graph structure, called a "Fuzzy Cognitive Map" (an "FCM"), is one example of such mechanism [5, 6, 7 & 8]. FCMs are fuzzy-graph structures that provide an expressive and flexible method of capturing and representing complex relationships in an intuitive manner. In case of an intuitive activity such as risk management, the FCM naturally represents the "human" way of thinking.

The risk management methodology presented in this paper employs FCM's to represent the relationships between the various security related issues to be effected in a specific phase in a cognitive and intuitive way. An FCM consists of nodes, which, in turn, represent the *issues that may occur to some degree*, and edges that describe the *relationships* (causal flow) between these issues. One of the activities that form part of the risk-analysis stage is determining the strengths of these relationships. The relationships have "fuzzy" strengths in the interval range [-1,1]. The strength of a relationship indicates the degree to which one issue affects another. These strengths are determined intuitively. We need to determine the strengths of all relationships depicted by the edges in the FCM. Consider figure 4 below:

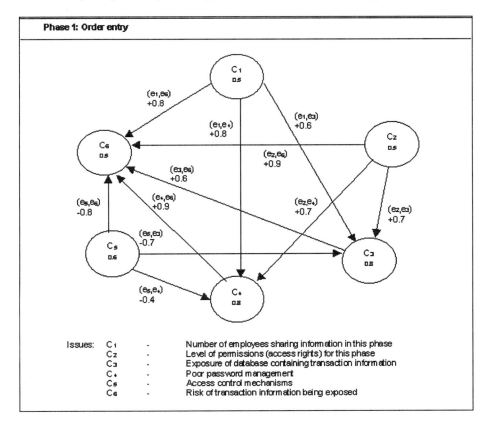

Figure 4. FCM representing the relationships between the security related issues that play a role in the order entry phase

A number attached to the respective edge indicates the strength of a relationship. Consider the relationship between the risk of transaction information being exposed (C_6) and the number of employees sharing that transaction information (C_1). The *plus 0.8 relationship* between C_1 and C_6 implies, for instance, that if the number of employees sharing transaction information during the order entry phase were to increase, then the risk of transaction information being exposed during this phase would also increase by a degree of 0.8, that is, by 80%. If, by the same token, the number employees were to decrease, then the risk of transaction information being exposed would also decrease to the tune of 80%. The strength of the relationship between the number of employees sharing transaction information and the risk of transaction information being exposed is, therefore, 0.8. The other plus relationships work in the same way.

The minus relationships, on the other hand, indicate the possibility of one issue increasing while decreasing another issue, and vice versa. In this way, the minus 0.7 relationship between C_5 and C_3 implies that if the strength of access control mechanisms implemented for the order entry phase were to increase, then the likelihood of database files containing transaction information being exposed would decrease to the tune of 70%. The reverse is also true: if the strength of these access controls were to decrease, then the likelihood of database files containing transaction information being exposed would increase by a degree of 70%. The strength of the relationship between the access control mechanisms and the exposure of database files containing transaction information is, therefore, 0.7. The other minus relationships works in the same way.

The final step in constructing the FCMs involves the specification of a trigger threshold for each issue. Such a trigger threshold (indicated by the number in the concept node that represents the issue) specifies the minimum strength to which the incoming relationship degrees must be aggregated in order to trigger the 'issue'.

Consider the following example: If the organisation is small, only a few employees, and the access rights allocated only include read and update, then it can be argued that poor password management would not be critical. This might be as a result of a culture of high trust (small company) and the policy of least privilege (read, update). However, if the organisation decides to increase the number of employees and allocate advanced access rights, such as append and delete, poor password management is critical and increase the risk significantly. The FCM implements this as follows: In order for C_4, poor password management, to be triggered, the incoming relationships must be aggregated to a minimum of 0.8, that is, 80%. If, for example, the level of access privileges for obtaining access to the transaction were to increase (C_2) and an increasing number of employees were to share the transaction information (C_1), then the incoming relationships (e_1,e_4) and (e_2,e_4) need to aggregate to at least 0.8 in order for the "poor password management" (C_4) issue to be triggered. The thresholds of the other issues are determined in the same way. Like the strengths of the relationships between issues, the trigger thresholds are also determined in an intuitive manner.

3.3.1 Construct edge matrices for the FCMs (Stage 4 task 4.3)

A simple two-dimensional *edge matrix* can be used to represent the strengths of the relationships between issues. Following, an example of an edge matrix in figure 5:

	C_1	C_2	C_3	C_4	C_5	C_6
C_1	0	0	0.6	0.8	0	0.8
C_2	0	0	0.7	0.7	0	0.9
C_3	0	0	0	0	0	0.6
C_4	0	0	0	0	0	0.9
C_5	0	0	-0.7	-0.4	0	-0.8
C_6	0	0	0	0	0	0

C_1 -	Number of employees sharing information in this phase
C_2 -	Level of permissions (access rights) for this phase
C_3 -	Exposure of database containing transaction information
C_4 -	Poor password management
C_5 -	Access control mechanisms
C_6 -	Risk of transaction information being exposed

Figure 5. An edge matrix representing the strengths of the relationships between the various issues that take place during a critical phase (order entry)

The i_{th} row lists the connection strength of the edges (e_i,e_k) *directed out* from issue C_i. The first row in the matrix indicates, for example, that the strength of the relationship (e_1,e_3) between C_1 ("Number of employees sharing information in this phase") and C_3 ("exposure of database files") is 0.6, that the strength of (e_1,e_4) between C_1 and C_4 ("Poor password management") is 0.8 and that the strength of (e_1,e_6) between C_1 and C_6 is 0.8.

Furthermore, C_i causally increases C_k if $(e_i,e_k) > 0$, decreases C_k if $(e_i,e_k) < 0$ and has no effect if $(e_i,e_k) = 0$. Event C_1 ("Number of employees sharing information in this phase"), for example, causally increases events C_3 ("exposure of database files"), C_4 ("Poor password management") and C_6 ("risk of transaction information being exposed") to varying degrees, because (e_1,e_3), (e_1,e_4) and (e_1,e_6) are all-greater than 0.

3.3.2   Construct "What-if scenarios" (Stage 4 task 4.3)

The edge matrix of the FCM can be used to *explore various "What-if" scenarios* in order to determine a way in which either to decrease such risk value or to explore whether or not a certain scenario would increase the risk value.   What would happen if, for instance, poor password management becomes a problem?   "What-if" scenarios such as these need to be constructed for this purpose.

Supposing that the IT risk value for a certain phase was calculated at 450 (on a scale of 0 to 1 000).   Each issue in an FCM triggers one or more other issues on (1) or off (0).   In order, for example, to model the "What-if" scenario, namely what would happen if, for instance, poor password management becomes a problem, event C_4 ("Poor password management") needs to be turned on, that is, to be set equal to 1.   All other events remain at 0 (remain unchanged).

This input state can be represented by the state vector [0 0 0 1 0 0], in other words, each issue (node) in the FCM is represented by either a zero or a one in the state vector, depending on whether it be turned on or off.   In our "What if" scenario, therefore, only the fourth element (representing C_4) in the state vector has a value of 1.   FCM input states such as these fire all the relationships in the FCM to some degree.   This process will show how, in a fuzzy dynamic system, causal events (issues) affect each other to some degree as time goes by.

In order to model the effect of the input state $I_0 = $ [0 0 0 1 0 0] ("Poor password management") on the FCM for the order entry phase along the *order-entry-and-delivering-of-goods* transaction information route, the following technique is used to determine the new state (on or off) for each event C_i each time (t_{n+1}) an input state fires the FCM.

$$C_i(t_{n+1}) = S(\sum_{K=1}^{N} e_{ki}(t_n)C_k(t_n))$$

This technique involves a matrix vector multiplication to transform the weighted input to each event (issue) C_i.   In the above equation, $S(x)$ is a bounded signal function, indicating whether C_i be turned off (0) or on (1) [6].

The above equation is applied to the FCM with initial input state [0 0 0 1 0 0] (that is, C_4, "Poor password management ", is turned on) as follows:

$I_0 = [0\ 0\ 0\ 1\ 0\ 0]$, then

$$I_0 E_c = [\sum_{k=1}^{6} I_{0k}e_{k1}, \sum_{k=1}^{6} I_{0k}e_{k2}, \sum_{k=1}^{6} I_{0k}e_{k3}, \sum_{k=1}^{6} I_{0k}e_{k4}, \sum_{k=1}^{6} I_{0k}e_{k5}, \sum_{k=1}^{6} I_{0k}e_{k6}],$$

where I_{0k} refers to the kth element in the state vector $I_0 = [0\ 0\ 0\ 1\ 0\ 0]$
e_{k1} refers to the entry in the kth row in the *first* column of the edge matrix E
e_{k2} refers to the entry in the kth row in the *second* column of the edge matrix E, and so forth.

$$= [0*0 + 0*0 + 0*0 + 1*0 + 0*0 + 0*0,$$
$$0*0 + 0*0 + 0*0 + 1*0 + 0*0 + 0*0,$$
$$0*0.6 + 0*0.7 + 0*0 + 1*0 + 0*-0.7 + 0*0$$
$$0*0.8 + 0*0.7 + 0*0 + 1*0 + 0*-0.4 + 0*0$$
$$0*0 + 0*0 + 0*0 + 1*0 + 0*0 + 0*0$$
$$0*0.8 + 0*0.9 + 0*0.6 + 1*0.9 + 0*-0.8 + 0*0]$$
$$= [0\ 0\ 0\ 0\ 0\ 0.9] \xrightarrow{0.5} I_1 = [0\ 0\ 0\ 1\ 0\ 1]$$

The arrow represents a threshold operation, with 0.5 the assumed threshold value. In other words, all entries in the state vector $I_0 Ec$ with values higher than or equal to 0.5 are turned on. In addition, C_4 is kept on, since we want to model the effect of a *sustained* threat of "**Poor password management**" being exposed during the order entry phase.

The following conclusion can, therefore, be made: when I_0 fires the FCM (that is, when I_0 occurs), then event C_6 ("the risk of transaction information being exposed") is turned on. The next input state firing the FCM will, therefore, be $I_1 = [0\ 0\ 0\ 1\ 0\ 1]$.

The equation formulated earlier is applied to the FCM with input state I_1 in the same way:

$$I_1 E_c = [\sum_{k=1}^{6} I_{1k}e_{k1}, \sum_{k=1}^{6} I_{1k}e_{k2}, \sum_{k=1}^{6} I_{1k}e_{k3}, \sum_{k=1}^{6} I_{1k}e_{k4}, \sum_{k=1}^{6} I_{1k}e_{k5}, \sum_{k=1}^{6} I_{1k}e_{k6}]$$

$$= [0\ 0\ 0\ 0\ 0\ 0.9] \xrightarrow{0.5} I_2 = [0\ 0\ 0\ 1\ 0\ 1] = I_1$$

This results in C_6 remaining on. The next input state $I_2 = [0\ 0\ 0\ 1\ 0\ 1]$ is, therefore, equal to the previous input state I_1. For this reason, the FCM converges to a fixed point I_2 that turns on C_6 ("the risk of transaction information being exposed"). This means that "Poor password management" in the order entry phase would increase the risk of transaction information being exposed (C_6).

The reader is referred to [6] for more information on this technique.

The foregoing example illustrates how an edge matrix constructed from an FCM can be used to explore "What-if" scenarios.

3.4   Identify the security services and controls (Stage 4 task 4.4)

Modelling "What-if" scenarios by making use of FCMs can, naturally, greatly facilitate decisions on the implementation of security controls for a specific phase along a transaction information route.

Consider the previous example, which hinges upon the exploration of a "What-if" scenario. The outcome of the scenario was that poor password management would indeed increase the risk of transaction information being exposed. The *confidentiality* of the transaction information would, therefore, be under threat. Furthermore, an unauthorised person gaining access to transaction information could also alter such information, thereby compromising its *integrity*.

In the foregoing example, confidentiality and integrity have been identified as the security services being under threat as a result of poor password management. It is essential in this case, therefore, to implement security controls in order to protect the confidentiality and integrity of the transaction information during the phase under consideration. For example, security controls such as improved password management and/or biometrics could be implemented in order to secure the transaction information.

3.5   Compile a report to this effect and obtain management approval (Stage 4 task 4.5)

Before the necessary security controls could be implemented, however, a report would have to be compiled in order to verify the need for such controls. The report must then be submitted to management in order to obtain its approval of the proposed security controls.

3.6   Devise a project plan (stage 4 task 4.6)

Only after management has approved the said report could a project plan be devised.

4.   CONCLUSION

This paper has been devoted to the presentation of a risk-management methodology specifically developed for assessing and analysing risks incurred by the business transactions of an organisation. The aim of the methodology is to enhance risk management by following a cognitive fuzzy approach to the assessment and analysis of risks. The advantage of using this approach is that the intuitive nature of human observation, which forms the basis of any risk assessment, and the vagueness regarding the decision-making process with respect to securing transaction information, are both taken into account when assessing and analysing IT risks.

The risk-analysis (fourth) stage of the methodology has been discussed in detail in this paper. The principal aim of this stage was to help manage risks by facilitating the decision-making process. This was achieved by first identifying the **critical phases** (that is, the high-risk phases) along each transaction information route by using the risk values calculated for each phase during the risk-assessment stage. Having identified these critical phases, **the critical transaction information routes** (high-risk transaction information routes) could be identified by aggregating the risk values of all phases comprising the specific transaction information route. In this way, the **high-risk areas** in an organisation can be pinpointed.

Furthermore, the cognitive fuzzy-modelling approach followed by the proposed methodology also enables the investigation of these critical areas with a view to enhancing the level of information security. This is achieved by making use of an FCM and by constructing various "What-if" scenarios to determine which of them might lead to the increase/decrease of a risk incidence. In this way, the decision-making process with respect to enhancing the overall information security is facilitated.

We aim our further research at developing a prototype to illustrate the functioning of the risk analysis stage and to prove that the model is not merely a theoretical concept, but that it can indeed be implemented successfully.

5.   LIST OF SOURCES CONSULTED

[1] LABUSCHAGNE, L. 1992. "Inligtingsekerheid, met spesifieke verwysing na risiko-ontleding." Rand Afrikaans University. Johannesburg, South Africa (dissertation (MCom) – RAU).

[2] PFLEEGER, C.P. 1997. Security in computing. United States of America: Prentice-Hall International Inc. 574 p.

[3] BADENHORST, K.P & ELOFF, J.H.P. 1989. Framework of a methodology for the life cycle of computer security in an institution. *Computers & Security*. 8: 433-442.

[4] ELOFF, J.H.P. & SMITH E. 2000. Cognitive fuzzy modeling for enhanced risk assessment in a health care institution. IEEE Intelligent systems & their applications. 15(2): 69-75.

[5] COX, E.D. 1994. The fuzzy systems handbook: A practitioner's guide to building, using and maintaining fuzzy systems. Boston: Academic Press. 515 p.

[6] KOSKO, B. 1997. Fuzzy engineering. New Jersey: Prentice-Hall. 549 p.

[7] KOSKO, B. 1986. Fuzzy cognitive maps. *International Journal of Man-machine Studies*. 24: 65-75.

[8] COX, E.D. 1995. Fuzzy logic for business and industry. Massachusetts: Charles River Media Inc. 601 p.

A SECURITY METHOD FOR HEALTHCARE ORGANISATIONS

MATTHEW WARREN AND WILLIAM HUTCHINSON[Ω]
School of Computing & Mathematics, Deakin University, Geelong, Victoria, Australia
[Ω]*School of Management Information Systems, Edith Cowan University, Perth, Western Australia, Australia.*

Key words: Security Management, Implementation, and Users.

Abstract: The use of participational approaches to system design has been debated for a number of years. Within this paper we describe a method that was used to effectively design information systems and implement computer security countermeasures within an healthcare environment and shown how it was used in a number of environments.

1.   INTRODUCTION

There are now many different types of Information Systems in place in the world, from transaction processing systems to decision support systems. All of these have one thing in common is that they require security. An issue is how can you implement technology including security into an organisation. An example method that can be used is ETHICS (**E**ffective **T**echnical and **H**uman **I**mplementation of **C**omputer based **S**ystem). The work on ETHICS was undertaken by Enid Mumford of the Manchester Business School, UK   (Mumford, 1983a). It is this participatory (also referred to as a socio-technical) approach that focuses upon people and procedures. This socio-technical approach is defined as "one which recognises the interaction of technology and people and produces work systems which are both technically efficient and have social characteristics which lead to high job satisfaction" (Mumford, 1983b). This paper introduces the SIM-ETHICS framework, which was used as part of a European Union IT and within Australia.

2.   THE SIM-ETHICS METHOD

The actual ETHICS methodology is a 15 level approach (Mumford, 1986) which details the steps needed to implement technology within an organisation. To try and overcome the problems of implementing security a new management methodology based on ETHICS was developed called SIM-ETHICS (SIM stands for Security Implementation Method). The philosophy behind SIM-ETHICS is that computer security is not only a technical problem but also involves organisational issues (Warren, 1999). The following are the steps used in the SIM-ETHICS method:

1) Initial Committee Consultation
The committee will be made up of a cross section of staff directly involved or affected by the implementation of the new security features. For example (Mumford, 1983a):

- representatives of staff from the different departments affected by the change;
- representatives of the IT department;
- representatives of the other users who will be using the new security systems.

2) Managerial consultation
The intended security countermeasures are evaluated against the SIM-ETHICS criteria to determine the level of impact its implementation will have. The criteria relates to (Warren, 1999):

- *Ease of Implementation;*
- *Training Issues;*
- *User Impact;*
- *Organisational Impact;*
- *Human Issues.*

At these meetings, issues relating to the introduction of the security systems would be discussed (as determined in Stage 1) as well as any other possible problems that managers could foresee.

3) Committee Stage
The views of the managers are discussed within the committee. It is now that initial problems are discussed, e.g. problems of introducing new security swipe cards.

The committee decides on how to approach the user consultation stage, such as:

- what questions to ask, for example, how do you feel about having to use new security swipe cards;
- the type of user to be questioned, for example, ward clerk;
- the number of users to ask, for example, every ward clerk.

4) Users consultation
A representative of the committee then meets the users to explain the proposed security countermeasures and then ask them a series of pre-set questions. The security countermeasures are then re-evaluated against the SIM-ETHICS criteria to take into account the newly raised user issues.

5) Committee Stage
The views of the users are discussed. If problems are found concerning the system, ways would be discussed on how to overcome the problem, e.g. increase the level of training.

6) Post implementation review
This meeting takes place after the implementation to determine if any unforeseen problems have occurred and if so discuss ways in which to rectify them.

3. RESEARCH OUTCOMES

SIM-ETHICS was used to determine the impact of two new security countermeasures (Warren, et al, 1995) within a major UK hospital. This major hospital was located in the South of England and was used as part of the European Union SEISMED (Secure Environment for Information Systems in Medicine) project. The hospital was used as a reference centre for the implementation of new security systems. The lessons learned from the implementation were shared with other partners within the project consortium. Based upon the SIM-ETHICS analysis the management of the hospital undertook the following actions:

Access Swipe Cards

Altered the staff training program by training key trainers from the separate departments. These key trainers would then train the rest of the staff in their department. A general promotion campaign was organised within the hospital to raise awareness of the new system and answer many of the commonly asked questions.

User Perception of Passwords

A general promotion campaign was organised within the hospital to raise security awareness especially when it was found that staff shared passwords and wrote them on the back of their ID badges.

SIM-ETHICS has also been used as part of a computer security risk analysis methodology called ODESSA (Organisational DEScriptive Security Analysis) and is used to determine the security requirements of healthcare organisations (Warren et a, 2000a). Any security countermeasures that are being implemented will effect the healthcare organisation as a whole. The SIM-ETHICS method is used to give management feedback on how security measures will impact an organisation (Warren, 2001). An example screenshot is shown at figure 1.

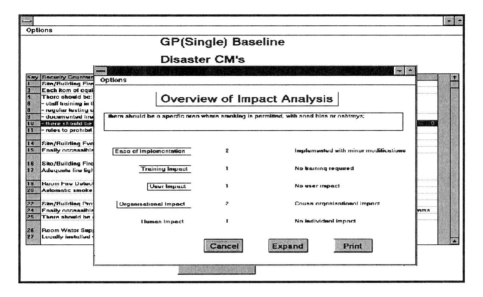

Figure 1. SIM-ETHICS analysis of Security Countermeasure

4.   SIM-ETHICS 2000

The major problem relating to SIM-ETHICS was that the evaluation criteria needed to be fully developed and used with new technologies e.g. impact of the Internet upon Security Management. It was decided to use the SIM-ETHICS method within Australia. The first step was to determine if there was a need for security within Australian hospitals. A computer crime survey was sent out to 60 IT Security Officers, who were based within hospitals in the state of Victoria, Australia (Warren et al, 2000b). There were 22 valid responses, giving a response rate of 37%. We will look at some key questions of that survey. In relation to Question 5 – "Has your Healthcare establishment performed a formal assessment to determine potential areas of risk?" A significantly higher number of private hospitals had undertaken such a review (66% compared to 34%). The majority of the private healthcare establishments had reviews undertaken by professionals within the establishment. Most of the public healthcare establishment used security consultants. The use of risk analysis is considered one of the most basic steps in identifying security threats that an organisation faces and implementing security countermeasures to protect against those security risks (Warren, 1997). Many Victorian hospitals are not implementing this basic step. Question 6 was a follow on from question 5, asking establishments if they had a formal written policy concerning computer security and the misuse of facilities. 64% of the public hospitals had a policy compared to 77% of private hospitals. The areas the policy covered were very similar for both private and public although more private hospitals responded that the policy covered "network intrusions" and "penalties for staff found committing computer crimes". Again the use of security policy is considered a basic step in developing a security culture, and surprisingly, one third of HCE did not have this in place. The survey provided that there was a potential need for a method such as SIM-ETHICS within Australia. One of the problems of the SIM-ETHICS method was there was a clear need to develop an appropriate evaluation mechanism. The following feedback criteria was developed to allow for the evaluation of security methods and allow for more focused feedback.

Within Australia there is a move towards the implementation of electronic healthcare records and allowing for on-line access to patient medical information. The Australian state of New South Wales is planning to implement such an on-line system by the year 2003. Each patient would have a single Unique Patient Identifier and use this with a password to gain access to their medical records (NSW Government, 2000). As the on-line medical system has not been developed yet, it was decided to evaluate the security requirements of a very similar style of on-line system. Web-CT is an on-line teaching system that is widely used by Universities to run courses. It allows students to remotely access the system and access their student records and post queries on discussion boards (as shown by Figure 2). The authors felt that this would be a suitable system to try and use the evaluation criteria.

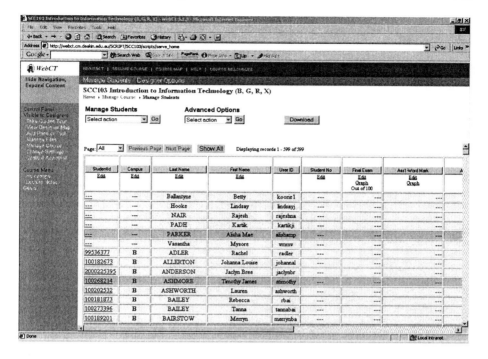

Figure 2. Example of Web-CT System

It was decided to evaluate a unit that contain 600 students and the review would look at how security could be implemented within the Web-CT system. The following is the outcome of the SIM-ETHICS review of that countermeasure using the evaluation criteria:

a) Impact of Security Mechanism
Implemented with minor modifications to existing systems or with the minimal amount of effort.

Points Raised:
The Web-CT system comes with built in passwords and each student is given a unique password (similar to a Unique Patient Identifier) to gain access to the system. There were some issues relating to giving passwords to new students.

b) Training Issues
No training requirements.

Points Raised:

Users were able to use the system very easily once they had their unique password.

c) User Impact
Countermeasure affects user satisfaction and caused a minor impact.

Points Raised:
Users were able to use the system very easily once they had their unique password.

d) Security Impact
Major Problem

Points Raised:
Once users had logged onto the system they could not log-out. This meant even though they thought they had finished a session, someone else could use the computer after them and access their Web-CT account. There is a danger that a user could masquerade as another user and post false messages to the discussion boards.

e) Human Issues
Results in restructuring a persons job or changing a persons individual power.

Points Raised:
Students could use a new technology in order gain access to their materials.

Outcomes
A message was posted on the Web-CT discussion board detailing the security fault and ways to deal with it such as clearing the Internet browser history file.

In this simple example we have assessed a similar systems to an on-line medical information system. We have proven in this case that the evaluation criteria work and posted warnings to the users about the security problem that was found.

A warning was posted on the Web-ct system describing the security weakness and ways to overcome the problem such as clearing the browser history or deleting the computers internet cache. The users then replied to the posting, raising a number of new issues that has not been considered such as:

- some users did not how to delete browser history or deleting the computers internet cache;

- the problem only affected certain types of browsers e.g. Internet Browser and not Netscape Communicator.

In conclusion the use of SIM-ETHICS 2000 has shown that a less structured method of SIM-ETHICS can be used to resolve problems quickly as well as ensuring full user participation and perhaps more importantly allowing feedback directly from the users after the review.

5.   CONCLUSIONS

The use of SIM-ETHICS has successfully enabled management to collect the consensus view of users relating to new security systems and has given management the chance to implement solutions to future problems, before they occurred. We have shown that the method can work within a European or Australian environment. The new evaluation criteria that has been developed will be used to increase in validity. The method gives management and staff information about problems that may occur, but it is the role of management to decide how to use this information when making decisions.

References

Mumford, E (1983a) *Designing Participatively*, Manchester Business School, UK, ISBN 0-903808-29-3.

Mumford, E (1983b) *Designing Human Systems*, Manchester Business School, Manchester, UK.

Mumford, E (1986) *Using computers for Business*, Manchester Business School, Manchester, UK.

NSW Government. (2000). *Report of the NSW Health Council – A Better Health System for NSW*, ISBN 0-7347-3138-8, Australia.

Warren, M.J. (1997) A new hybrid approach for Risk Analysis, *In Proceedings of IFIP WG11.1 - Information Security Management Conference,* Copenhagen, Denmark, May.

Warren, M.J. (1999) *A Practical Soft System Management Approach to Implementing Security*, Deakin University Technical Report CC99/05, Deakin University, Australia.

Warren, M.J (2001) *A Risk Analysis Model to reduce computer security risks among healthcare organisations*, Risk Management: An International Journal, Vol 3: No 1, pp 27-37, Perpetuity Press, UK.

Warren, M.J, Gaunt, P.N (1994) SP11-06: The use of SIM-ETHICS at a UK Health Authority, *European Union SEISMED Research Report SP11-06*.

Warren S, Warren M.J (2000). The Role of Participation in Systems, *In Proceedings of International Conference on Systems Thinking in Management, (Incorporating the First Australasian Conference on System Dynamics and Sixth Australia and New Zealand Systems Conference),* Geelong, Australia, November.

Warren, M.J, Warren, S, Love, P.E.D (2000a) Using Participation Effectively to Implement and Evaluate Information Security within an Organisation, *In Proceedings of Americas Conference on Information Systems 2000 (AMCIS 2000).* Long Beach, California, USA, August.

Warren S, Hutchinson, W, Warren M.J (2000b), Healthcare IT Security: Can the European Union experiences assist Australia, *In Proceedings of ACIS (Australasian Conference on Information Systems) 00,* Brisbane, Australia, December.

INTERPRETING COMPUTER-RELATED CRIME AT THE MALARIA RESEARCH CENTER
A Case Study

GURPREET DHILLON[1] and LEISER SILVA[2]
[1]*College of Business, University of Nevada, Las Vegas, NV 89154, USA Email: dhillon@ccmail.nevada.edu*

[2]*Department of Accounting and MIS, University of Alberta, Edmonton, T6G 2R6, Canada Email: Leiser.Silva@ualberta.ca*

Key words: Computer-related crime, computer fraud, computer ethics, business ethics, self-regulation, self-control.

Abstract: This paper assesses issues concerning management of computer-related crime. It argues that organizations that focus exclusively on formal regulatory measures in business management fall short of protecting their resources. The argument is conducted by analyzing the pre and post computer-related crime situation at the Malaria Research Center. Findings from the case study suggest that ethical managerial behavior can not be cultivated by strict rule structures but through self-regulation. The paper uses Gottfredson and Hirschi's (1990) theory to evaluate the case. In a final synthesis the paper illustrates how inappropriate control measures can adversely affect the integrity of an organization.

1.   INTRODUCTION

Any occurrence of computer-related crime is a matter of grave concern for an organization and often leads to disastrous consequences. Organizations however tend to deal with computer-related crime situations in a reactive mode, building on short term solutions rather than identifying long term options or the negative consequences of their actions. It is important therefore to analyze all possible causes and effects. The extent of the problem can be gauged from various surveys and reports that show marked increase in computer-related crime situations and the related protection measures. According to a report in The New York Times (Chen 1998), in 1996 companies spent $830 million on information security technology to guard against potential abuses. In the same year the Computer Security Institute survey found 42% of Fortune 500 companies reporting computer-related crimes (New York Times 1997). A subsequent study in 1999 by the Computer Security Institute reported losses amounting to nearly $124 million (theft of proprietary information $42.5 million; financial fraud $39.7 million; laptop theft $13 million). Similarly a 1997 British study by the Audit Commission found organizations reporting computer-related fraud to have increased from 34% in 1994 to 45% in 1997.

Computer-related crime is not just one type of crime; it is a ubiquitous variant of all crime. Parker (1983) contends that ultimately this variant will become a dominant form. Indeed, the myth of computer related crime has become so distorted and exaggerated that the real problems are not being addressed. According to Sieber (1986), such real problems relate to the "precise knowledge of the rapid changes regarding the phenomena and characteristics of computer crime". This paper is an attempt to understand the problems concerned with managing computer-related crime. It argues that organizations that focus exclusively on technical and formal control measures in their systems, fall short of protecting their resources. Hence it is argued that organizations should focus more on the pragmatic control measures (for other research sympathetic with this viewpoint see (Dhillon 1997; Hitchings 1996). The argument of this paper is conducted by analyzing the computer related crime situation at the Malaria Research Center. The case illustrates how inappropriate control measures can affect the integrity of an organization.

2.   PRIOR RESEARCH

Literature suggests that white-collar crimes are spontaneous and opportunistic acts and that offenders are not really in control of their behavior (e.g. see Croall 1992; Hester and Eglin 1992; Taylor *et al* 1992). More often however, criminal behavior typically entails considerable detailed preparation. This contention would appear at odds with popular misconceptions where white-collar criminals are portrayed as habitual losers, scratching out a miserable existence by taking extreme risks or are too lazy and stupid to do anything else. Numerous studies have shown that those who commit occupational crimes tend to be exactly the kind of people companies would want on their pay roll (Parker 1983; Ball 1990). In fact Parker (1983) maintains that these individual are "almost always young, energetic, highly motivated and intelligent".

Research in white-collar crime can broadly be classified into three categories. First are those researchers who have focused exclusively on the personal factors of an individual. These researchers argue that most criminal activities arise because of the personal situation of the offenders. Croall (1992) for example considers greed to be the prime cause of criminal behavior. On the other hand Cressey (1986) links crime to personal, non-sharable financial problems. Indeed there is a positive correlation between the personal factors of an individual and incidents of crime. Clinard's (1983) research based on retired middle management executives supports this contention.

The second category of researchers is those who consider work situation as a determinant of criminal acts. In the literature it has been argued that low pay and oppressive working conditions often lead employees to get involved in criminal activity. Scraton and South (1984) for example argue that since operational level workers are often subjected to a high level of surveillance they often end up becoming disgruntled. As a consequence they have a greater probability of becoming involved in a crime. Furthermore, even minor offences by operational staff are less tolerated than by those who are high up in the management hierarchy. While explaining the opportunities afforded by the work situation, Carroll (1982) suggests that any criminal act is inherently rational. Therefore most offenders weigh the possible consequences of their actions and take advantage of the criminal opportunity only if it is in their interest to do so. A similar viewpoint is propounded by Clarke (1985). He defines an initial involvement model of crime. This model acknowledges the impact of psychological, sociological and environmental determinants in the conduct of a criminal activity.

In the third category are researchers who consider criminal activity to be arising from the socio-organizational environment. The socio-organizational environment is closely reflected by the organizational structure. It has been argued that the risk of criminal activity increases with the complexity and the geographical spread of a corporation (e.g. see Aubert 1977; Braithwaite 1985; Clarke 1990; Croall 1992). Typically subsidiaries of an organization can be used by the top management to circumvent control at the operational level. A common denominator in managing computer-related crime in an organization, irrespective of its size or geographical spread, is the quality of its management. This is because most crimes are committed through collusion or compliance of management and staff. It has been reported by Clinard (1980) that nearly 40% of the large corporations had no record of any offence. It therefore follows that the culture of an organization plays an important role in the performance of a criminal act. Such cultures and normative structures in an organization take form from the technological and social work organization and the senior management attitudes (e.g. see Croall 1992; Mintzberg 1983; Dhillon 1999).

Poor quality of management and inadequate management communication has often been considered as cornerstones of an unethical environment. Most organizational workplaces are characterized by such predicaments. The importance of establishing an ethical environment within an organization cannot be overstated. Forester and Morrison (1994) maintain that there is little doubt that the ethos of certain work environments is conducive to crime. Much of the responsibility for organizational ethics lies with senior managers for it is they who form the particular style that influences so many aspects of corporate behavior. Hearnden (1990) contends that "an unequivocal management attitude and a clear statement about what constitutes acceptable behavior vis-a-via (say) expense claims or private telephone calls, will help to set the parameters for employee behavior over a range of issues".

An organizational climate that adopts trust-based relationships encourages individuals to take responsibility for their actions. Trust, in this context, is considered to mean consistency and integrity, the feeling that a person or organization can be relied on to do what they say. Since every job embodies some element of trust, organizations could well harness this feeling and thus enhance employees' self esteem. When control and restrictions replace trust and confidence, the whole organization will experience disruption.

3.   THEORETICAL BASE

In this paper we adopt the theoretical framework proposed by Gottfredson and Hirschi (1990) to describe and evaluate the case study. Gottfredson and Hirschi emphasize the importance of instituting individual restraint on the behavior of people. The notion of 'self-control' is central to Gottfredson and Hirschi's general theory of crime. The importance of self-control is qualified on basis of three tenants. First that people differ in extent to which they are compelled to undertake a criminal act. Second that criminal acts require no special capabilities, needs or motivations. Third that lack of self-control allows almost any deviant, criminal, exciting or dangerous act. These three principles form the basis for describing the nature of self-control and the related individual characteristics that result in a criminal act. Gottfredson and Hirschi contend that the nature of the individual characteristic can be derived by understanding the nature of the criminal acts. As will become evident in the following sections, the Malaria Research Center case study describes a particular criminal act and we use Gottfredson and Hirschi's principles to interpret the nature of the characteristics. Doing so helps us to identify the kind of controls that could have been put in place within the Research Center.

Based on Gottfredson and Hirschi's theory, table 1 summarizes various elements of interest in any crime situation. In subsequent sections these elements are used to tease out computer-related crime issues in the Malaria Research Center case study. It is our endeavor to understand different dimensions of the problem - on the one hand the characteristics of the individuals involved in a criminal act and on the other the management response in dealing with the situation. In the final synthesis it will be possible to draw interpretations from a real situation for good practice.

When interpreting the nature of gratification of desires, we are confronted with two dimensions - temporal and simplicity. The temporal dimension suggests that criminal acts provide an almost immediate gratification of desires and hence people with low self-control have a tendency to respond to substantial inducement. Since these people concern themselves with the immediate environment, they tend to have a very concrete orientation exclusively confined to the situation at hand. The second dimension deals with easy or simple gratification of desires, suggesting that the people with deviant behavior tend to be involved with acts that provide money without work and hence have very little persistence in a course of action.

The nature of consequences is another important element in Gottfredson and Hirschi's theory. It is contended that people with little self-control tend to be adventuresome, active and physical. Nature of consequences has also been posited as one of the primary components in Jones' (1991) moral intensity model. The general theory of crime considers cognitive requirements of a criminal act to be minimal and hence people lacking self-control do not necessarily possess or value cognitive or academic skills. Criminal acts also do not require any manual skills. It follows therefore that people with little self-control do not have any manual skills that require training.

The nature and scope of benefits from a criminal act (magnitude of benefits) form another dimension of the Gottfredson and Hirschi's theory of crime. They suggest that since crimes result in few or meager benefits, they are not necessarily equivalent to career or a job. Hence people with low self-control tend to have an unstable job profile and seem to be uninterested in long-term occupational pursuits. Criminal acts also result in pain or discomfort for the victim. As a consequence property is often lost, bodies are injured, privacy is lost and trust is broken. People with low self-control therefore tend to be self centered and insensitive to the feelings of others.

Table 1. Elements of interest in Gottfredson and Hirschi's general theory of crime

Gottfredson and Hirschi's self-control elements	Predictions by Gottfredson and Hirschi's General Theory of Crime	Low self-control expressions
Nature of gratification	Criminal behavior result in: Immediate gratification Easy or simple gratification of desires	People with low self-control: Respond to tangible stimuli in the immediate environment Have a 'here and now' orientation Look for money without work, lack diligence, tenacity or persistence
Nature of consequences	Criminal acts are exciting, risk thrilling	Criminal acts involve stealth, danger, speed, agility, deception, or power
Nature of planning and magnitude of benefits	Little skill or planning is needed for performing criminal acts Crimes result in: Few or meager benefits Pain or discomfort for the victim	People lacking self-control need not possess or value cognitive or academic skills People with low self-control tend to be little interested in and unprepared for long-term occupational pursuits People with low self-control tend to be indifferent or insensitive to the suffering and needs of others

4. THE CONTEXT OF THE MALARIA RESEARCH CENTER CASE

This section presents a case study of illicit activities at the Malaria Research Center, a research organization associated with the United Nations. The field research was carried out at the headquarters of the organization during 1995/97. A total of 30 formal in-depth interviews were conducted with various groups within the organization (senior managers, middle managers and employees in supportive roles). Interviews were also carried out with an ex-employee of the Research Center. This helped in validating the findings. The logical form of the interviews was based on a topic guide, the content of which was drawn from previous related research and Gottfredson and Hirschi's general theory of crime. Topic guides were customized for each interview. During data collection, the theoretical aspects of computer related crime were kept separate from the actual case (i.e. interpretations were made only after data collection). This prevented personal bias from influencing data collection (as suggested by Walsham 1995; Symons 1991). Based on the traditions of qualitative research, the methodological approach was interpretive in nature. Discussion of an interpretive research paradigm is beyond the scope of this paper. However the theoretical aspects of interpretive research can be found in Walsham

(1993) and Orlikowski & Baroudi (1991). Application and examples of interpretive research designs can be found in the works of Dhillon (1997), Serafeimidis (1997) and Madon (1991).

The Research Center was set up at the behest of the Malaria World Wide Research Organization (MWRO). Ever since its conception, the Research Centers' mission has been to investigate problems associated with malaria and other tropical diseases across the globe. The head of Research Center is the Director, appointed directly by MWRO. Given that the Research Center is governed by two separate organizations (MWRO and the Directive Council, constituted of health ministers of member countries) the process of decision-making is very complex. The organizational structure at the Center is matrix thus resulting in multiple reporting lines. For example, a person working on a specific research project, might report to three different roles: the project manager, the head of the technical division and the co-ordination offices. Supervision, as in many academic and research organizations, is based on responsibility rather than by putting pressure on employees.

The two main areas in which the Research Center faces competition are technical co-operation and research. While competition on research comes from both universities and the Non Governmental Organizations (NGO), competition on technical co-operation is mainly from the NGOs. In fact, these competitive forces question the very existence of the Research Center. The decision-making process for negotiating a research project is inflexible.. Small NGOs, however, can reduce overhead costs and without a complex organization, as in the case of the Research Center, negotiations with donors are more straightforward. However the most serious problem at the Research Center was the discontinuous nature of the budget. It was project based and hence there was no guarantee that jobs could be maintained after work on a particular project was completed. Such a situation resulted in instability and uncertainty among staff members.

During 1994-95 the budget was reduced by approximately 40%. As a consequence a large number of staff at the Research Center were made redundant. This drastic reduction in personnel resulted in low morale among staff members. Although the Director adopted certain measures to rectify the situation, discussions with various staff members revealed that the Director had been slow in recognizing the problem. The researchers had regularly complained that the internal administration of the Center was not only too expensive (averaging approximately at US$ 600,000 a year) but also inefficient. Given the inherent complexity within the Malaria Research Center, the following sections explore as to how various organizational measures fell short of maintaining the overall integrity. Elements drawn from Gottfredson and Hirschi's general theory of crime are used to review various aspects of the case.

5. INTERPRETING THE NATURE OF GRATIFICATION

Gottfredson and Hirschi posit nature of gratification as one of the determinants of self-control in a given situation. When interpreting the nature of gratification, the general theory of crime stresses on 'immediacy' and 'ease' dimensions (i.e. how immediately or easily can criminal acts provide gratification of desires). The paragraphs below describe a situation at the Research Center and interpret it on basis of the two dimensions of gratification.

Background

Because of the composite nature of the administration at the Research Center, i.e. being administrated by MWRO and receiving funds from donors, and competing in the marketplace, clearance of accounts was a very complex process. However the administrative procedures in place were complex and not very cost effective. This resulted in a significant budgetary deficit. As a consequence the donor agencies got concerned about the manner in which the Research Center was administered. In 1989 MWRO appointed a new administrator whose main mission was to reduce the deficit by implementing tighter administrative controls.

Easy gratification of desires at the Malaria Research Center

The new administrator saw the development and implementation of a computer-based information system as a means to achieve administrative efficiency. The information system was also seen as an effective way to institute new control structures. It was decided that the new information system would eventually substitute an obsolete system that was believed to be one of the most notorious culprits of the deficit. The old system was running on a mini computer bought in the 70s and it was programmed in a traditional procedural language. The new information system was to be implemented on a microcomputer network and programmed in a fourth generation language. The Director of the Research Center thought that the administrative information system was exclusively a matter for the administration and therefore did not intervene in its design or development. With total control over the new information system, the administrator decided to launch the system in 1990. The new information system centralized and controlled majority of the operations – ranging from the purchase function (from computers to laboratory reactives) and the hiring of new staff. Once the system was in place many researchers complained about it, indicating that the new controls were in fact an obstacle in performing their day to day activities. The researchers pointed out that the administration had ignored their information needs while developing the system. Since at the time of system analysis and design the task of reducing the deficit was the main priority for the Center, the complaints were dismissed with indifference.

Immediate gratification of desires at the Malaria Research Center

By the end of 1990, the deficit had not yet been reduced and MWRO became impatient and continuously kept sending auditors to the Research Center. One such mission in January 1991 discovered something wrong in the accounting books particularly those related with computer purchases and the payment of staff health insurance. Nobody within the Research Center had questioned the transactions since the whole process had been computerized. The main problem was that a number of computers registered on the books were greater than those actually existing on site. Given that the computers bought were cheap clones, the prices listed in the accounting books were excessively high in comparison with market prices. Furthermore, even though a computer system aimed at increasing efficiency had been implemented; the payment of health insurance was being made one month late. The auditors established that in fact the money was being deposited in a bank account to earn interest in favor of the administrator and that the insurance company had agreed to receive their payment thirty days later. The auditors also discovered that the computer hardware provider was a closed friend of the administrator and that the insurance company had agreed to give a month's credit as an incentive for 'winning' in the tendering process, which of course was controlled by the administrator. Clearly the administrator would have not been capable of doing this without full control on the analysis, design and management of the information system.

6.   NATURE OF CONSEQUENCES AT THE MALARIA RESEARCH CENTER

Gottfredson and Hirschi suggest that people involved in criminal acts are shortsighted in their orientation. They do not necessarily consider all the pros and cons prior to getting involved in a criminal act. This contention is evidenced in the Research Center case. Clearly the administrator lacked self-control and exhibited typical traits of being adventuresome and not being cautious. Obviously the administrator was not interested in maintaining the long-term viability of the institute. This becomes clear from the sequence of events described below.

In February 1991 the administrator was asked to leave the Research Center. He had been formally discharged on grounds of fraud. The administrative charge of the Research Center was taken up by MWRO. A new administrator was appointed at the end of the intervention whose mission was not only to reduce the deficits but also to eradicate corruption. She introduced even tighter controls. Instead of making the administrative information system flexible, it was transformed into a 'bureaucratic toy'. As a consequence of the intervention, by explicit orders of MWRO, the authority of the Director was curtailed. The Director was no longer entitled to purchase goods whose prices were above five thousand US dollars. Director's responsibility for authorizing permanent contracts was also dissolved. Furthermore the director was not even entitled to authorize trips beyond the limits of the immediate geographical region.

The difficulties in conducting business at the Research Center are exacerbated by the fact that MWRO headquarters were very slow in responding to most of the requests. As a result of the intervention, contracts of research projects and the acceptance of donations although negotiated by the Director of the Center could only be authorized by MWRO. However, the most serious damage was the reputation and credibility of the Research Center. Soon after the intervention the respective governments, competitor NGOs and donors undoubtedly questioned the trustworthiness of the Research Center and were concerned of their association. The intervention also had serious consequences in the social integration of the Center. Although the new administrator was eventually able to reduce the deficit and there were no incidents of fraudulent behavior, the price paid was high. The Center resulted in having centralized and extremely despotic administrative processes. The administrative information system, instead of facilitating organizational processes, was an obstacle in achieving the objectives of the research projects. This resulted in the alienation of the research staff. Over the past five years, the administrators and the research staff have constantly been pointing fingers at each other. As a consequence most research projects fail to finish on time and end up being over budget. The context of the Center is such that it will not be long when the losses will amass and the organization will face a financial crisis.

We are not claiming that the fraud committed in the Research Center was the cause of all organizational and economic problems of the Center. However, we cannot deny that the social and material price paid as a consequence of the crime is very high. Had the frauds not been committed, the Center could have saved a lot of time effort and resources. Most importantly the Research Center would have retained its autonomous position. Indeed computer-related crime has effects that go beyond the disappearance of goods and resources. In fact organizations and jobs might disappear as a consequence of it.

7.   NATURE OF PLANNING AND MAGNITUDE OF BENEFITS AT THE MALARIA RESEARCH CENTER

When understanding the nature of planning and magnitude of benefits at the Research Center, the interpretations seem to be at odds with the argument proposed by Gottfredson and Hirschi (1990) in their general theory of crime. Gottfredson and Hirschi recognize the shortcoming when they note, "the concept of white-collar crime is usually seen as incompatible with most theories of crime" (pg 196). The general theory of crime suggests that usually little skill or planning is needed for criminal acts. Furthermore crimes provide few or meager long-term benefits. The situation at the Research Center was to the contrary. The situation at the Center suggests that computer related crime is a rational act, since the crime was committed by an internal employee who typically evaluated two key factors. First, the likelihood of being caught. Second the severity of the punishment if the crime is detected.

The traditional means to contain computer-related crimes has focused on increasing the probability of detection. Invariably this demands extra controls to be instituted in any organization. In the case of the Center, such controls have made the information system virtually unusable. This means that perhaps more appropriate means of curtailing computer-related criminal activities need to be put in place. Indeed Bologna (1984) suggests that a good means to secure organizational assets is to shift the concentration of cost and effort from physical controls to decreasing the probability of commission. This calls for a shift in the mindset in terms of dealing with criminal activities within organizations. If we analyze the control systems in place within the Research Center, after the fraud facilitated by the computer system had taken place, we see that an excessive thrust had been placed on the technical and formal measures.

When the new administrator was appointed, one of the fears of the organization was to curtail any occurrence of crime. This resulted in a number of overt control measures being instituted. In general, control measures correspond to the level of criminal activity. Dhillon (1998) suggests criminal activity to occur at the input, throughput or output stages. Input crimes are typically committed by entering false or manipulated information into the computer systems. The throughput frauds generally take the form of 'salami slicing'. Output crimes are generally committed by either concealing bogus inputs or by postponing detection. Since within the Research Center the computer-related fraud had taken place at input and output levels only, most of the controls were formal bureaucratic ones. Informal discussions with different individuals within the Research Center however revealed that it was really the management practices and personnel policies that should have been addressed. This raises an interesting question of establishing a balance between the more pragmatic measures against the formal and technical controls. This is a strategic issue that needs to be addressed at a corporate level. Provided that an organization begins to consider the more human/behaviorist countermeasures, the management focus then would be on decreasing the probability of commissioning of a fraud. This will be in contrast to the earlier focus on decreasing the probability of occurrence. At the Research Center, with the appointment of a new administrator, organizational thrust was definitely on minimizing occurrences of fraud. This may not necessarily be the desired option. On the other hand, if the organizational thrust is on decreasing the probability of commissioning of a fraud, management attention shifts towards other softer issues. Such softer issues may include aspects of self restraint and inducement restraint, something that was absent at the Research Center. If attention is paid to these softer concerns, promotion of self-esteem of individuals and the development of an ethical culture are facilitated.

The management at the Research Center has been reactive in dealing with the post computer-related crime situation. The implementation of overt controls by the new administrator perhaps resulted in feelings of oppression, which in turn leads to disaffection among employees. Since previous research has shown that internal employees of the organization pose the greatest threat (e.g. see Dhillon 1999; Brown 1991; Audit Commission 1994), the Research Center is potentially vulnerable to further criminal activity. In order to manage the Research Center better and to decrease the probability of commissioning of a crime, the focus should be on building a high level of trust that incorporates the deterrence doctrine. The inherent argument of such an approach is that an environment, which embodies high levels of trust between management and employees, acts to reduce the need for excessive management controls. Self-control becomes the dominant ethos, rather than imposed control. The overall strategy encompasses two principal techniques, individual/group self-control and good organizational practices.

Lessons learnt

Based on the study presented in this paper, two broad categories of lessons can be learnt. The first lesson pertains to the practical importance of inculcating a culture of self-control within organizations. Gottfredson and Hirschi's (1990) theory of general crime supports this contention. The second lesson is methodological in nature and is concerned with the advantages and disadvantages of using the general theory of crime in this study. Both these lessons are discussed below.

The notion of individual and group self-control adopts proactive mechanisms, which encourage self-restraint. Research done by Hollinger and Clark (1983) has identified a positive correlation between certainty of detection and severity of punishment in the reduction of levels of theft. Empirical evidence from the retail sector supports Hollinger and Clark's contention (e.g. see McNees 1976; McClaughlin 1976). In the context of managing computer related crime, a focus on self and inducement restraint will result in discrete, though explicit warnings to employees that all breaches of security will not only result in instant dismissal but also criminal prosecution. Moreover employees should be encouraged to report instances of security breaches that they encounter. This can be reinforced by linking salary increases or productivity bonuses to levels of security breaches. The aim should be to promote the notion that honesty rather than dishonesty brings rewards. Since employees are deemed to act rationally, the assumption is that they will seek to obtain the maximum benefit. In the case of the Center, although the old administrator was dismissed instantly, no criminal proceedings were initiated. Furthermore, no effort was made to encourage employees to be part of the drive to curtail computer related criminal activities. At the Center, although it was a high ranking official who had been involved in the crime, the resultant controls in the management procedures and the information system had a more direct effect on the lower level employees. Discussions with various people in the organization revealed that most employees of the Center were not entirely happy with the way the business was conducted. They felt that they were being left out from all major decision making exercises and were not informed of the latest developments. It should be remembered that since majority of the Center employees are highly qualified individuals, the existing work practices within the organization would result in these individuals becoming dissatisfied, disillusioned and disgruntled. This may become a potential source of further computer related criminal activity, especially because it is these people who come in contact with the information system on a regular basis.

Although Gottfredson and Hirschi (1990) claim that their theory has general applicability, evidence coming from the Research Center case suggests that the general theory of crime falls short in explaining certain kinds of white collar crime. Although the theory was useful in interpreting the nature of gratification and consequences, it fell short of making accurate predictions about the nature of planning and the magnitude of benefits. Nevertheless the arguments proposed by the theory were helpful in analyzing the Research Center situation. Clearly further case study research is needed to validate the usefulness of the conceptual framework presented in table 1.

Prior research in testing the general theory of crime has largely taken a quantitative mode of inquiry (e.g. see Evans et al. 1997). This research uses qualitative case based interpretive research as a means of understanding a computer related crime situation. Qualitative case based studies are beneficial in developing an in-depth insight into particular situations. However they have often been subjected to criticism for their lack of generalizability. However the intention of this paper is not to draw generalizations. Rather it aspires to present a descriptive understanding of a given situation. This is done by borrowing a 'lens' (i.e the theory proposed by Gottfredson and Hirschi 1990). There are limitations in doing so as Walsham (1993) comments "theory is both a way of seeing and a way of not seeing" (p6). Provided a researcher is aware of the limitations, such problems can be overcome. Future research directions certainly demand a further review of the general theory of crime in interpreting other computer-related crime situations.

8. CONCLUSION

At a practical level this paper has shown the limitations of a misguided confidence placed in technical and formal control measures while protecting organizational resources. In doing so the paper has highlighted the importance of more pragmatic measures. Such measures have been related to good management practices and management communication. In addressing the issue of computer related crime, this paper has suggested that the management will have to institute changes in its attitudes, values and corporate working environment. Therefore by focusing on the more pragmatic measures it is possible to build in high levels of trust. In using Gottfredson and Hirschi's (1990) concepts qualitatively, this paper makes a methodological contribution to computer-related crime literature. The paper also identifies certain weaknesses in the general theory of crime to explain certain white-collar crime situation. Further investigation in this area is warranted for.

9. REFERENCES

Aubert, V. (1977). *White collar crime and social structure*. The Free Press, New York.
Audit Commission, (1994) Opportunity makes a thief. Analysis of computer abuse, The Audit Commission for Local Authorities and the National Health Service in England and Wales.

Ball, L. (1990). Computer crime. In: *The information technology revolution*. T. Forester, Ed. Basil Blackwell, Oxford.

Bologna, J. (1984). *Computer fraud: the basics of prevention and detection*. Butterworth, London.

Braithwaite, J. (1985). White collar crime. *Annual Review of Sociology*(11): 1-25.

Brown, R. K., (1991) Security overview and threat, National Computer Security Educators, Information Resource Management College, National Defense University, Washington DC, Tutorial Track, NCSC.

Carroll, J. (1982). Committing a crime: the offenders decision. In: *The criminal justice system: a social psychological analysis*. V. Konecni and E. Ebbesen, Eds. Freeman and Company, San Francisco.

Chen, D. (1998) Man Charged With Sabotage of Computers. *New York Times*, February 18, 1998.

Clarke, M. (1990). *Business crime: its nature and control*. Polity Press, Cambridge.

Clarke, R. and D. Cornish (1985). Modeling offenders decisions: a framework for research policy. *Crime and Justice - An annual review of research* 6: 147-185.

Clinard, M. B. (1983). *Corporate ethics and crime*. Sage Publications, Beverly Hills.

Clinard, M. B. and P. C. Yeager (1980). *Corporate crime*. The Free Press, New York.

Cressey, D. (1986). Why managers commit fraud. *Australian and New Zealand Journal of Criminology* (19): 195-209.

Croall, H. (1992). *White collar crime*. Open University Press, Milton Keynes, UK.

Dhillon, G. (1997). *Managing information system security*. Macmillan, London.

Dhillon, G. (1998). Choosing appropriate organizational controls: managing the information assets. In: *Effective utilization and management of emerging information technologies*. M. Khosrowpour, Ed. 473-477. Idea Group Publication, Hershey PA.

Dhillon, G. (1999). Computer crime: interpreting violation of safeguards by trusted personnel. In: *Managing information technology resources in organizations in the next millennium*. M. Khosrowpour, Ed. 602-606. Idea Group Publishing, Hershey.

Evans, T. D., F. T. Cullen, et al. (1997). The social consequences of self-control: testing the general theory of crime. *Criminology* 35(3): 475-504.

Forester, T. and P. Morrison (1994). *Computer ethics: cautionary tales and ethical dilemmas in computing*. The MIT Press, Cambridge.

Gottfredson, M. R. and T. Hirschi (1990). *A general theory of crime*. Stanford University Press, Stanford, California.

Hearnden, K. (1990). Computer crime and people. In: *A handbook of computer crime*. K. Hearnden, Ed. Kogan Page, London.

Hester, S. and P. Eglin (1992). *A sociology of crime*. Routledge, London.

Hitchings, J. (1996). A practical solution to the complex human issues of information security design. In: *Information systems security: facing the information society of the 21st century*. S. K. Katsikas and D. Gritzalis, Eds. 3-12. Chapman & Hall, London.

Hollinger, R. and J. Clark (1983). Deterrence in the workplace: perceived certainty, perceived severity and employee theft. *Social Forces* 62(2): 398-418.

Jones, T. M. (1991). Ethical decision making by individuals in organizations: an issue-contingent model. *Academy of Management Review* 16(2): 366-395.

Madon, S. (1991). The impact of computer-based information systems on rural development: a case study in India. Ph.D. Thesis. University of London, .

McClaughlin, T. (1976). A proposal for a behavioral approach to decrease shoplifting. *Corrective and Social Psychiatry* **22**: 12-14.

McNees, M. e. a. (1976). Shoplifting prevention: providing information through signs. *Journal of Applied Behavioral Analysis* **9**: 339-405.

Mintzberg, H. (1983). *Power in and around organizations.* Prentice-Hall, Englewood Cliffs.

New York Times. (1997) Big eight Ministers meet on international computer crime. , 12 November.

Orlikowski, W. J. and J. J. Baroudi (1991). Studying information technology in organizations: research approaches and assumptions. *Information Systems Research* **2**(1): 1-28.

Parker, D. (1983). *Fighting computer crime.* Charles Scribner's Sons, New York.

Scraton, P. and N. South (1984). The ideological construction of the hidden economy. *Contemporary Crises* (8).

Serafeimidis, V. (1997). Interpreting the evaluation of information systems investments: conceptual and operational explorations. Ph.D. thesis In: *Information Systems Department.*: London School of Economics and Political Science, University of London, London.

Sieber, U. (1986). *The international handbook on computer crime.* John Wiley & Sons, Chichester.

Symons, V. J. (1991). A review of information systems evaluation: content, context and process. *European Journal of Information Systems* **1**(3): 205-212.

Taylor, I., P. Walton, et al. (1992). *The new criminology: for a social theory of deviance.* Routledge, London.

Walsham, G. (1993). *Interpreting information systems in organizations.* John Wiley & Sons, Chichester.

Walsham, G. (1995). Interpretive case studies in IS research: nature and method. *European Journal of Information Systems* **4**(2): 74-81.

INTRUSION DETECTION SYSTEMS:
Possibilities for the Future

KAREN A. FORCHT

Andersen Consulting Professor of CIS
CIS/OM Program, College of Business, James Madison University, Harrisonburg, VA 22807,
FORCHTKA@JMU.EDU, 540-568-3057(o)

CHRISTOPHER ALLEN
4001 Alabama Avenue, NE, St. Petersburg, Florida 33703

BARBARA BRODMAN
Rt. 2 Box 385, Kents Store, Virginia 23084, (804) 589-3418, gpfbab@mindspring.com

DAVID CORNING
14 Tideview Drive, Dover, New Hampshire 03820, (603) 749-7816, davidcorning@msn.com

JACOB KOUNS
3201 Copper Mill Trace, Apt. L, Richmond, Virginia 23294, (804) 747-3279,
jkouns@bellatlantic.net

Key words: Intrusion detection systems, artificial intelligence, neural networks, operating systems   audits, passive protocol analysis, network-based ID systems, signature detection, network interface card, black box, firewall, viruses, Trojan Horse.

Abstract: Man has used Intrusion Detection Systems since the dawn of time. The systems that have been developed for detecting and monitoring Information systems are becoming more accepted as an integral part of security solutions. There are limitations in the success rate and usefulness of the systems in use, however, there are some exciting developments on the horizon. By combining artificial intelligence, neural networks and similar advances in programming, we can look forward to Intrusion Detection Systems that will not only raise the alarm, but take the appropriate action to thwart the attack.

1.   INTRODUCTION

The term IDS is fairly new, born out of the cyber world's attraction to anagrams, but the concept of Intrusion Detection Systems has existed since the dawn of time. Organisms developed immune systems designed to detect the existence of unwanted intruders and later, man expanded the use of Intrusion Detection Systems beyond the confines of the human body. Domesticated dogs were used to identify potentially dangerous intruders and then later trained to protect herds. Ever since man has had something of value to protect, Intrusion Detection Systems were used. Today, what we need to do is protect information systems. To do this, we have developed a digital watchdog to protect us from the virtual "wolves" in cyberspace.

1.1   Networking of Computers

The widespread use and networking of computers has created an environment where valuable information can be stolen or sabotaged without a physical presence and with unprecedented stealth. Much like the need to protect important items in the real world, similar security measures must be taken on the digital level to protect our valuables in cyberspace. Intrusion detection is an important component of a security system, and it complements other security technologies. By providing information to site administration, ID allows not only for the detection of attacks explicitly addressed by other security components (such as firewalls and service wrappers), but also attempts to provide notification of new attacks unforeseen by other components. Intrusion detection systems also provide forensic information that potentially allows organizations to discover the origins of an attack. In this manner, ID systems attempt to make attackers more accountable for their actions, and, to some extent, act as a deterrent to future attacks.

1.2   Systems

In general, ID systems are used to detect unauthorized usage or misuse of a computer system. This is done by analyzing and scrutinizing operating system audit trails that form a footprint of system usage and then look for sequences of transactions that suggest suspicious activity. Using this passive protocol analysis, ID systems can identify suspicious activity by recognizing known attack patterns and through statistical behavior anomaly detection (the recognition of deviations from normal activity). ID systems can monitor at both the network and host level and these very often are used in conjunction.

1.3   Network-based Systems

Network based ID systems are designed to detect unauthorized activity throughout a network by monitoring all network traffic passing on the segment where the agent is installed and reacting to any anomaly or signature-based suspicious activity. Host-based ID systems analyze the activity on a particular computer. They can detect attacks that are not detectable by network-based ID systems since they can view events local to a host.

IDS's analyze events using two techniques: 1. signature detection and anomaly detection and 2. honey pots. Signature detection monitors for activity that matches a predefined set of events that are known to be an attack. Signature-based, therefore, must be specifically programmed to detect each known attack. Anomaly-based ID systems find attacks by identifying unusual behavior (anomalies) on a host or network. Anomaly-based IDS defines normal behavior based on a statistical profile or normal usage. It then monitors the host or network to find use that deviates from this defined normal behavior. See Figure 1.1

Characterization of Intrusion Detection Systems Based on Data Source

Host based
Audit data from a single host is used to detect intrusions.
Multihost based
Audit data from multiple hosts is used to detect intrusions.
Network based
Network traffic data, along with audit data from one or more hosts, is used to detect intrusions.

Characterization of Intrusion Detection Systems Based on Model of Intrusions

Anomaly detection model
The intrusion detection system detects intrusions by looking for activity that is different from a user's or system's normal behavior.

Misuse detection model
The intrusion detection system detects intrusions by looking for activity that corresponds to known intrusion techniques (signatures) or system vulnerabilities.

©Comstock 2000

Figure 1.1

1.4   Decoy Systems

Complementary to the IDS is the use of Honeypots. Honeypots act as a decoy that appears to have several vulnerabilities, making it attractive to hackers. Set up to look like a legitimate system with legitimate files, the Honeypot will lure the intruder and he/she will believe the information residing there is important. The hope is that the hacker will stay involved with the Honeypot long enough to discern the information about the intruder and the source of the attack necessary to capture him. However, the primary purpose of the Honeypot is to monitor and learn from the intrusion so systems engineers can determine how the systems were exploited. This information can be used to prevent attacks on real systems. Since the Honeypot should have no other role, any connection attempt to it should be suspicious. (See Figures 1.2, 1.3, 1.4)

1.5   A Basic Network Security Model

Firewalls are not enough

Due the historical minimal effectiveness of Network based ID systems, companies have not yet embraced them, thinking that a Firewall will provide sufficient security. To completely protect an organization however, audits of the network on a regular basis are a necessity.

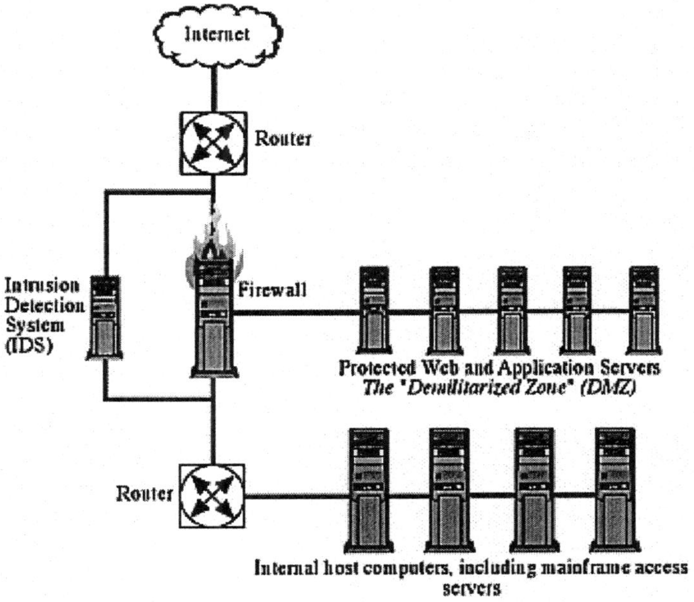

Figure 1.3

Network Based Intrusion Detection

Network based IDS's are those that monitor traffic on the entire network segment. A Network interface card (NIC) can operate in one of two modes, these being:

Normal Mode, where packets which are destined for the computer (as determined by the Ethernet or MAC address of the packet) are relayed through to the host system.

Promiscuous mode, where all packets that are seen on the Ethernet are relayed to the host system.

A network card can normally be switched from normal mode to promiscuous mode, and vice-versa, by using a low-level function of the operating system to talk directly to the network card to make that change. Network based intrusion detection systems normally require that a network interface card be in promiscuous mode.

Figure 1.4

1.6   Characteristics of a good Intrusion Detection System

An Intrusion Detection System should address the following issues, regardless of what mechanism it is based on:

1. It must run continually without human supervision. The system must be reliable enough to allow it to run in the background of the system being observed. However, it should not be a "black box". That is, its internal workings should be examinable from outside.
2. It must be fault tolerant in the sense that it must survive a system crash and not have its knowledge base rebuilt at restart.
3. On a similar note to above, it must resist subversion. The system can monitor itself to ensure that it has not been subverted.
4. It must impose minimal overhead on the system. A system that slows a computer to a crawl will simply not be used.
5. It must observe deviations from normal behavior.
6. It must be easily tailored to the system in question. Every system has a different usage pattern, and the defense mechanism should adapt easily to these patterns.
7. It must cope with changing system behavior over time as new applications are being added. The system profile will change over time, and the IDS must be able to adapt.

2.   EXISTING SYSTEMS

Many choices for Intrusion Detection Systems exits, including those that cost tens of thousands of dollars and those that are free. InfoSec Managers need to view those choices within a cost/benefit environment. Understanding these systems and their capabilities is necessary to provide the most cost effective protection.   Additionally, most IDS systems only work with one operating system so there are Unix and Windows based IDS's. These usually operate in conjunction with a firewall.

2.1   Unix-Based Systems

Unix has several host based systems each covering different areas.

- The first is **TCP Wrappers**. This program does not change existing configuration files and does not increase overhead. The Wrappers log the name of the existing client host and the requested service. Each packet is logged with a timestamp. When a service is requested (Ftp, Systat, Finger, Telnet etc.). The Wrapper checks its access control list and, if permitted, engages the service. If the connection is not allowed, the packet is dropped and a log entry written.

- **Tripwire** is a program that monitors system files and any file that has been tampered with can be detected. The program uses a cryptographic hash that changes if the file has changed. When a file has been changed, an email alert is sent to provide notification. Tripwire cannot prevent a file change but merely notifies that one has occurred.

- **CMDS** is a log file reader. It builds a profile of systems and reports activity that varies from that norm. It has a capacity to spot new attacks better than signature systems as it does not rely on a catalog of known attacks but logs changes to the system.

2.2   Windows NT Systems

Windows NT suffers from a variety of threats mostly viruses and Trojan Horses. Here are a few NT host based Intrusion Detection Systems.

- **NukeNabber** is the Windows equivalent of TCP Wrappers. This program can identify scans and collect the IP address of scanners. NukeNabber is able to block certain ports to traffic as well as monitor ports and collect data.

- **Back Orifice Friendly** is a program that is designed to detect Back Orifice (BO) probes. Back Orifice is essentially a remote administration tool that allows others to take control of your computer. Once BO is installed on a computer without a password, anyone with a BO program can scan the Internet and log onto an infected computer.

- Personal firewalls include **Zone Alarm, At Guard and BlackICE Defender**. These firewalls are installed on host computers and detect attacks from the outside as well as notification when applications are trying to connect from the inside.

- Network Based Intrusion Detection is designed to primarily detect attacks from the Internet. Most of the network systems are libcap based. Libcap is used to get information from the operating systems kernel. This deals with the granting of privileges and processes. Libcap then passes the information to the application.

- **Snort** is a lightweight IDS. It is capable of performing real time traffic analysis and packet logging. The program can detect buffer overflows, port scans, CGI attacks and OS fingerprinting attempts. It can be used as a packet scanner or packet logger.

- **Shadow** is a signature based detection system. The basic SHADOW setup is two systems: a data-collection machine known as a sensor, and an analysis station. The sensor sits on the network of interest and captures all the traffic. The raw data files are moved via a secure channel to the analysis station for inspection. Shadow is for Unix based systems.

- **Cisco Secure IDS** is a Unix-based system that features a sensor and a director. The sensor has alarms, which captures important information such as attack description, IP addresses and keystroke capture. Secure IDS is a signature system and can recognize a variety of attacks. The director is a transparent IDS and does not consume system resources.

- **ISS RealSecure** operates under NT and Unix systems. The system features an easy interface that uses red, yellow and green icons to signify alerts. This product also has a sensor and a console. RealSecure detects over 200 attacks but is known to generate false positives.

- **CyberCop Monitor** is a network-based system that monitors incoming and outgoing network traffic. It has a signature database of over 170 attacks and can alert to time spanned attacks. This product also suppresses Denial of Service (DOS) attacks and protects against unauthorized changes to system files.

3. FIREWALLS

Firewalls are the first line of defense for most networks. There are two types: 1. a packet filter that does a quick inspection of packets and 2. a stateful application gateway proxy, which can tear up packets and rewrite them. Firewalls are usually deployed at the point called the Demarc where the ISP's responsibility ends and the company network begins. Simply, firewalls are used to control the access to permitted types of traffic. Firewalls use Access Control Lists (ACL) to allow or deny packets to enter or leave the network. If a service or entrance is denied, the packet is dropped and not allowed to enter the network. The firewalls are configured using rule sets that can be permissive or restrictive. Security policies tend to be written documents that have no teeth but the firewall can enforce policies by allowing or disallowing events that the security policy prescribes. Of great use to InfoSec professionals is their logging feature. All events are logged and the perusal of logs can contribute greatly to understanding any attempted intrusions. One hides the network behind it. Firewalls also provide protection by providing a translation function. An internal network often has a different IP scheme than the one presented to the public. The firewall translates the external address into the correct internal address and delivers authorized packets to their destination.

4.   USER AUTHENTICATION

There is growing need to detect and prevent unauthorized activities both from within and outside an organization. User authentication and access control measures are limited and abusers are finding more and ever more clever ways to compromise such systems. Proactive monitoring of system activity along with immediate responses to a problem are the next best hope for improved Intrusion Detection (perhaps it will now be called Intrusion Detection and Response).

Intrusion Detection Systems will need to utilize Artificial Intelligence, Neural Networks and Expert Systems in order to reach full potential. Recently introduced **Retriever,** a newer product of Symantec Corporation is a proactive network security management tool capable of discovering and mapping network components. It also can identify vulnerabilities and perform network audits. What's new about this software is its ability to predict by performing network security modeling, like a "what-if" analysis and provide the solutions to fix them.

If an IDS sensor can "learn" its surroundings on the network, it will begin to make its own decisions. It will determine normal traffic and thus avoid false-positives. Most sensors simply report comparisons to stored signature files, enabling any signatures not in the database to remain unnoticed. After mapping the network, the IDS could then make intelligent decisions about the proper steps to take. These could be customizable and could include:

- Issuing of an explicit request (or challenge) for further authentication

- Recording of details in an intrusion log for later inspection/investigation

- Immediate notification of the system manager (alarm)

- Phased reduction of permitted behavior

- Locking of the intruders terminal

- Termination of the anomalous session.

4.1   Examples of Attacks

How does this differ from historically used ID systems? Recent attacks that have been detected have continued after the IDS thinks it has stopped. When a user on the Internet begins an attack, the IDS probe sees it and watches the session to determine if it's continuing or if it has stopped. The intruder, however, has manipulated the TTL (Time to Live) flag within a TCP packet and has set it to 1 less than it takes to reach the actual webserver. The packet is then sent out to close the attack, fooling the IDS probe into thinking it's over. Since the TTL of the packet is set one hop less that the webserver, it never makes it there and the attack continues. Mapping the network would allow the IDS probe to know exactly how many hops away all of the servers are located. Then, if this type of packet came in again with an altered TTL, it could realize the webserver did not reset the connection and that the attack is continuing.

Hackers continue to trick IDS probes to disable matching attacks with signatures. IDS probes need to implement "packet scrubbing", causing an alert whenever a command attempts to gain root.   Using Artificial Intelligence, the IDS could realize it needs to recompile fragmented packets before assessing the activity.

4.2   Expert Systems Examples

The use of a general expert system applied to Intrusion Detection has only recently been taken seriously. The reasons for this are related to low performance, difficult integration and language complexity. However, the Production-Based Expert System Toolset (P-Best) is sufficiently fast for real-time detection of attack methods such as SYN flooding and buffer overruns. It also is interoperable with OS libraries and easily integrated into anomaly and misuse detection. Providing strategies and mechanisms for understanding the state of a given environment, this can derive logical inferences that can lead to conclusions, such as deductive reasoning or bottom up reasoning.

P-Best is now being applied to the analysis of network traffic streams. It analyzes TCP/IP packet streams for low level layer attacks and higher layer attacks involving vulnerable network service layer protocols like FTP, SMTP and HTTP. An Internet accessible P-Best translation service that will allow users to develop and compile rule sets into self contained expert systems.

4.3 Artificial Intelligence

Artificial Intelligence is used to solve complex that are:

- Usually resolved by an expert

- Not amenable to straight forward solution by numerical computation; or, if they might theoretically be solved numerically, the computations would take an impractically long time and/or use too much computational resources

- Usually solved by people using rules of thumb (heuristics), that work most of the time but with no guarantees

- Ill-defined

- Related to situations that constantly change over time (i.e. are dynamic), so that a better solution is likely to be made by someone (or some software) that can take the changes into account as they happen, rather than set up rules for decision making in advance by trying to anticipate what changes may happen

- Not readily solvable by breaking the problem into interacting sub-problems

- Highly dependent on the context within which the problem occurs in terms of determining an adequate solution

"Artificial Intelligence is no match for natural stupidity"

-Anonymous

4.4 Active Evidential Reasoning

Active Evidential Reasoning, inspired by model-based reasoning, plan recognition and automated diagnoses systems in order to improve ID capabilities. ICE (Intelligent Correlation of Evidence) systems are capable of the detection and diagnosis of threats by correlating evidence from configuration examination, host audit data, network sniffers, agent-based evidence collectors and predictive analysis techniques. Using such diverse and redundant evidence sets allows the detection of intrusions by highly skilled hackers who try to conceal their actions. Also, after collecting corroborating and refuting evidence such a system can tune its internal models, resulting in fewer false alarms. The US Air Force's Rome Laboratory is researching these systems in order to add response to network Intrusion detection.

4.5   Neural Networks

Neural Networks process information the way biological nervous systems, such as the brain, do. Their basic concept is in the structure of the information processing system. Made up of many connected processing neurons, a neural network system uses the technique of learning by example to resolve problems. The neural network is configured for specific applications, such as pattern recognition, through a learning process called training. "Neural networks can differ on:

•   the way their neurons are connected

•   the specific kinds of computations their neurons do

•   the way they transmit patterns of activity throughout the network

•   the way they learn, including their learning rate

Neural networks are being increasing used to solve real world problems that are so complex that they do not have a defined algorithmic solution. Neural networks can solve problems people can solve. These include pattern recognition, forecasting and analyses.

4.6   Distributed Agents

Most Intrusion Detection Systems in large networks must use several distributed agents instead of one large module. These agents need to use artificial intelligence in order to handle the various intrusion problems. Using a Bayesian alarm network to work as an independent agent to narrow detection efforts to a specific type of the attack in a large network, such as a denial of service, worm or virus, would allow more knowledge about the attack within the system. Individual nodes of the network could develop their own model of the Bayesian alarm network and agents could communicate between themselves and with a common security database. Networks should be set up hierarchically so that the top level Bayesian alarm network that is interconnected to the lower level networks and data could substitute for a distributed Intrusion Detection System.

4.7   Inference Logic

Inference Logic for automated reasoning about misuse in computer and network operations is beginning to be realized and holds the greatest promise for IDS development. InfoSec Managers can look forward to a broad array of new products that will utilize these increasingly more usable systems for Security confidence.

Maintaining network security is not a serial process, and not a series of discrete steps, with 'security' being the end product. Previous security models have failed to properly emphasize the interdependence of the critical elements of the security process, hence, we use of the term "security ecosystem", rather than merely "security cycle" or "security wheel". The security ecosystem is a community of dynamic, evolving processes functioning as an organic unit that protects the network through a combination of preventative and proactive measures. An organization's security ecosystem should be a balance of the continuous processes of risk assessment (assess), network monitoring (monitor), risk countermeasures (respond), and policy review and enforcement (policy). If one of these critical elements is missing, or practiced sporadically, this will upset the balance that optimally exists between these processes.

5. REFERENCES

1. Escamilla, Terry. 1998. Intrusion Detection: Network Security beyond the Firewall. Wiley Computer Publishing.
2. Sams, Net. 1997. Maximum Security: A Hackers Guide to Protecting your internet Site and Network. Macmillan Computer Publishing.
3. Tipton, Harold F. and Krause, Micki. 2000. Information Security Management Handbook, 4th Edition. CRC Press.
4. SC Magazine. Buyers Bible 2001 . December, 2000. pp.48-62.
5. Bauer, R. Kenneth and Halme, Lawrence R. AINT Misbehaving: A taxonomy of Anti-Intrusion Techniques. SANS Institute Resources.
6. Intrusion Detection Primer.http:/www/linuxsecurity.com/feature_stories/ feature_store-8.html
7. Elson, David. Intrusion Detection, Theory and Practice.March 27, 2000 Securityfocus.com http://www.securityfocus.com/
8. Fried, Stephen. Information Security, The Big Picture. Sans GAIC 2000.
9. Furnell, Steven M. and Dowland, Paul S. A Conceptual Architecture for real time Intrusion Monitoring. Information Management and Computer Security. 8/2/2000. MCB University Press.
10. Hart, Rod; Morgan, Darren and Tran, Hai.An Introduction to automated Intrusion Detection Approaches
11. Information Management and Computer Security. 7/2/1999. MCB University Press
12. Hoglund, Greg and Gary, John. Multiple Levels of Desynchronization and other concerns with testing an IDS System. Updated August 11, 2000 http://securityfocus.com/frames/?focus=ids&content=/focus/ids/articles/desynch.html
13. Hartley, Bruce. Honeypots: A new Dimension to Intrusion Detection" http://www.advisor.com/MIS

14. Klug, David. Honey Pots and Intrusion Detection. September, 2000. SANS Institute Resources.

15. Lindqvist, Ulf and Porras, Phillip A. Detecting Computer and Network Misuse Through the Production Based Expert System Toolset (P-Best).Swedish National Board for Industrial and Technical Development.

16. Merkow, Mark. Standing Sentry Over Your Network update April 13, 2000. http://securityfocus.com/focus/ids/articles/markmerkow.html

17. Metaxiotis, K.S. and Samouilidis, J.E. Expert Systems in Medicine: academic illusion or real power? Information Management and Computer Security. 2000 MCB University Press.

18. Me and my SHADOW Using the new SANS intrusion-detection software with Solaris. http://www.sunworld.com/sunworldonline/swol-09-1998/swol-09-security_p.html

19. Northcutt, Stephen. Intrusion Detection, The Big Picture.Sans GAIC 2000.

20. Price, Katherine. Introduction to Intrusion Detection. 9/22/00. COAST http://www.cerias.purdue.edu/coast/intrusion-detection/ids.html

21. Thomas, Benjamin D. Intrusion Detection Primer. Linuxsecurity.com

22. Turrell, Timothy. IDS September 2000. SANS Institute Resources.

23. Intrusion Detection FAQ. http:www.sans.org/newlook/resources/IDFAQ/behavior_based.htm

24. http://www.home.cs.utwente.nl/~aps/IDS_onderzoek.shtml

25. http://www.cs.nps.navy.mil/people/faculty/rowe/idtutor.html

26. http://www.geek-girl.com/ids/0280.html

27. http://www.robertgraham.com/mirror/Ptacek-Newsham-Evasion-98.html

28. http://www.networkintrusion.co.uk/

29. http://csrc.ncsl.nist.gov/nistbul/itl99-11.txt

30. Continuous Adaptive Risk Management. Hiverworld, Inc. http://www.hiverworld.com/

31. http://www.secinf.net/info/ids/nn-idse/paperF13_2.html

32. Glossary of Artificial Intelligence Terms. SHAI http://www.shai.com/ai_general/glossary.htm

33. NSA Glossary of Terms Used in Security and Intrusion Detection. SANS Institute Resources. http://www.sans.org/newlook/resources/ glossary.htm

Implementing Information Security Management Systems
An Empirical Study of Critical Success Factors

FREDRIK BJÖRCK
Department of Computer and Systems Sciences

Stockholm University / Royal Institute of Technology

Electrum 230, SE-164 40 KISTA, Sweden

Phone (office) +46.8.6747498, (celluar) +46.70.7777917

Fax +46.8.7039023 ("Attn.: Björck")

Email: bjorck@dsv.su.se

Keywords: Information security management system, information security policy, IT security

Abstract: This paper presents the findings of an empirical study of certification auditors' and information security consultants' experiences and insights concerning the implementation and certification of information security management systems. Using an action research strategy and a grounded theory research method, the study describes these particular experiences and insights primarily in terms of critical success factors vital to the implementation and certification processes. Two tentative theoretical frameworks, providing synthesized views of these factors, are put forth.

1. INTRODUCTION

Implementation and certification of ISMS (information security management systems) currently interests many researchers and practitioners. Especially 7799 – the British and now also international standard for ISMS (ISO 2000, BSI 1999) - have received a lot of attention in the information security research community lately:

Siponen (2001) criticises 7799, and other information security (management) standards, from the viewpoint of philosophy of science and argues that these standards are were developed based on personal observations that were not scientifically justified. In addition, Siponen argues, the standards in question claim to be universally valid, although they are not.

Eloff and S. Von Solms (1998, 2000a, 2000b) suggests that both IT product security (measured by for example Common Criteria) as well as procedural information security (measured against for example 7799) have to be taken into account when measuring the level of information security in an organisation.

S. Von Solms (2000) declares that information security must be managed on both a macro and a micro level. The macro level (information security at an inter-organizational level) should be managed with the help of, and measured against, an internationally accepted framework, such as the 7799 standard. The micro level (information security at the intra-organizational level) should be managed through a dynamic measurement system. Furthermore, he argues that an information security certification scheme, such as those set up for 7799, should play an important role in the future.

R. Von Solms (1999) makes a business case for the standard using a metaphor of driving a car:

"Any motor vehicle on a public road requires a valid roadworthy certificate that will indicate that all technical safety and security mechanisms and features on the vehicle are present and functioning properly. The driver needs a driving licence that will indicate that he/she has learned how to drive the vehicle in a secure way by using the technical safety features correctly and effectively. Further, a third party, i.e. traffic officers, will continuously ensure that the vehicle is functioning technically well and also that the driver obeys all road usage regulations." (R. Von Solms, 1999)

He concludes that "...BS7799 can certainly provide the basis to ensure "safe driving on the information super highway" (R. Von Solms, 1999).

Labuschagne (draft, forthcoming) asserts that 7799 could rightfully be used as one of the cornerstones of web assurance in an electronic commerce context.

While many other authors have written about 7799, this is just to demonstrate that it receives a lot of attention. Although much has been written about the standard itself, very little has been written about the *practical application* of the standard. And so far, we have not found any published empirical studies on this subject – at least not related to the 7799 standard. Consequently, even though this study is somewhat limited in its scope and depth, it might still prove interesting for practitioner and academics.

The research question of this study is:

What are the critical success factors needed for successful implementation and certification of information security management systems?

This answer is sought after via an action research strategy and a grounded theory method.

2. RESEARCH STRATEGY AND METHOD

2.1 Research Strategy

An *action research* strategy is essentially defined by four characteristics; it deals with a (i) *practical* research problem in a (ii) *participatory* style. In addition, the pursuit of (iii) *change*, though a (iv) *cyclical research and feedback process*, is considered an integral part of research (Denscombe, 1998, p. 57). Even though we clearly follow this strategy, as will be clarified and justified here, the study was not really consciously designed or labelled as action research from the onset. In effect, the strategy was determined by the context in which the research took place. A brief examination of the four defining characteristics of an action research strategy clarifies this issue:

Practical. The study was carried out within the context the Swedish Standards Institutes' 7799 project, which aim was to translate the BS7799 standard (BSI 1999) into Swedish, and make it an official Swedish standard (SIS 1999). Since this aim was reached in June 1999, the focus of the project was shifted towards generating and sharing experiences and insights about ISMS implementation and certification. For this, a "pilot certification workgroup" was formed, aiming to guide a few organisations all the way from start to 7799-certification (Sweden has a similar certification scheme as the British one based on part 2 of the standard). We were invited to join this group as researchers, because there was a clear need for the experiences and insights to be documented and shared among the group members and in the Swedish information security- and business communities at large. Evidently, there was a practical problem: How do we go about implementing and certifying these management systems with little or no previous experience about 7799?

Participation. The pilot certification work group is unique in that it brings together certification auditors, information security consultants, government agencies, organisations interested in certification and researchers (us). All of these parties have been working together with the aim to generate and share the knowledge created. The respondents – the practitioners - have shared their own experiences and insights; we have merely summarized them in this study. They needed the knowledge themselves, that is why they decided to participate. We have participated in the pilot certification work group during the course of two years.

Change. A common understanding of what is required for the successful implementation and certification of ISMS according to the 7799 standard was sought. Moreover, we were looking for a methodology of *how* this can be done. The parties wanted to change - or calibrate - their views on these issues so as to research this consensus.

Cyclical feedback. For this change, mentioned above, to take place the results were (and still are) fed back by means of presentations of what we have learned, and through written feedback reports. There are three target groups for this feedback; the practitioners in the project (and in the study), the other information security and certification practitioners in Sweden, and the information security community at large – research as well as practice. This paper is also a part in this cyclical feedback loop.

We have now demonstrated that the strategy (i) was determined by the context in which the research took place, (ii) it can be labelled action research, and that (iii) it is reasonable for the study.

However, there are no research strategies without disadvantages – this is also true for action research. The main scientific objection to this kind of research strategy is probably that if can affect the "representativeness of the findings and the extent to which generalizations can be made on the basis of the results" (Denscombe, 1998, p. 65). This is true also for this study, but the objection assumes that the action research project takes place in only one organisation (a "work-site approach"). This study is concerned with experiences and insights from many organisations and many different contexts, which may make the results more universal. Another objection against action research is that the researcher most likely cannot be totally detached and objective in relation to the subjects under study, since s/he is so immersed. This is of course totally against the positivistic ideas as pointed out by for example Susman and Evered (1978). Nevertheless, it is also a scientific advantage since it gives the researcher a closer and deeper view of what is studied. Being aware of these problems and we have tried to stay as neutral as possible in the process of asking questions and analysing and making conclusions from respondents' answers.

2.2   Research method

While the high-level research strategy and context were that of *action research*, the more specific research method follows the ideas of *grounded theory* (Glaser & Strauss 1967, Strauss & Corbin 1994).

Two sets of questionnaires were developed and sent to the respondents. They were composed of open-ended questions, so as to not restrain the thinking of the respondents. Each form contained six questions, and they were slightly different for certification auditors and information security consultants. This paper only report the findings of one question, which was posed in exactly the same wording to both groups:

In your opinion, which are the critical success factors for a successful implementation of an information security management system, ISMS? (Please give reasons for your answer)

The questionnaires were written in Swedish, so this is a translation. Although the question does not explicitly refer to the standard as such and to the problems associated with the certification process, the respondents rightly read this into the question because of the context within which it was asked. That context is; that they were asked about their experiences and insights as members of the Swedish *7799* pilot *certification* group.

In total, there are 8 certification auditors and 18 information security consultants in the Swedish 7799 pilot certification group. All of these were asked to complete the questionnaire. The response rate for the certification auditors were 75% (`(6/8)*100`), and for the consultants 56% (`(10/18)*100`). We have not formally analysed why some decided not to answer the survey. However, we do know that most of the ones who have not answered are new members of the group. Being new, they are likely to have limited experience and insights about the exact question. This fact might explain why they did not answer.

The answers were ranging from single sentences to quite extensive explanations. The exact answers were imported into ATLAS/ti – a methodology support tool for qualitative analysis of data especially supporting a grounded theory methodology. The answers from the auditors and the consultants were analysed separately, and therefore they will be presented separately in this paper. The idea with this was to see if there were any differences in insights and experiences (and views) between these two groups.

Each answer was coded with a code describing its content. And then patterns were looked for in the data. A more specific description of the analysis is provided under each section below.

3.   CERTIFICATION AUDITORS' PERSPECTIVE ON IMPLEMENTATION AND CERTIFICATION OF ISMS

Once again, the question was stated as follows (translation from Swedish to English):

```
In your opinion, which are the critical success
factors for a successful implementation of an
information security management system, ISMS?
```

From the answers, we could distinguish six different success factors. Since the consensus was so profound, we chose to present the answers sorted after each factor- starting with the most important, or at least the most frequently mentioned factor. All the answers fell within these six categories.

The critical success factors for implementation and certification, from the perspective of the certification auditors were the following:

1) Management commitment

Support from the top management of the organization, and their commitment to and understanding of the problems of information security was seen as one of the most important success factors for an efficient implementation of ISMS. This factor was mentioned firstly by all of the respondents in this group (auditors), even though there were no fixed answer alternatives and despite the fact that the respondents were unaware of each other's answers. The following quotations speak for themselves:

"Top management's interest and commitment in its own ISMS project. ..."

"Top management's commitment and an understanding that the management system for information security must cover the whole business."

"Top management's commitment..."

"Top management's understanding and commitment, in deciding the security policy / security level and to participate actively in the risk analysis and the continuity planning."

"Top management's commitment. ..."

"Endorsement from the company's / organization's top management. ..."

2) Well-structured project

Another important success factor which was identified was that the ISMS implementation project in the organization is well-planned and –structured. The respondents expressed it like this:

"An organizational unit responsible for the totality and for the risk analysis which is the foundation for all activities. ..."

"... a well defined project with delimited sub-projects. ..."

"A well developed project plan and a correctly dimensioned project organization. ..."

Taken together, there are many aspects concerning the organization of the ISMS development and implementation that are mentioned:

- that the responsibility for the project is defined,
- that it is clear who shall carry out the different steps in the project
- that goals, resources and the time plan for the project are developed and documented in a project description, and
- that the resources in the project are well balanced.

3) Holistic approach

The project members – and other employees – ability to see the "full picture" is stressed by many of the respondents as an important success factor. Sometimes, it seems like the certification auditors have a feeling that the IT-technical aspects are handled in a very detailed way, but at the price to the detriment of obtaining a holistic view. Therefore, they meant that a more holistic approach and thinking in the projects should lead to positive consequences and pave the way to a more successful implementation and possibly certification of ISMS. Two of the respondents put it this way:

"...that the participants in the work with identifying the risks are representing the whole business, that is not only security but also other parts of the business."

"Understanding that the management system for information security must cover the whole enterprise."

As can be seen from the quotations, it is mainly the connection between the information security and the organizations core activities (processes) that is seen as important – that the ISMS does take into account and that it covers the whole organization – so that the ISMS does not end at the security- or IT department.

4) Appreciating the need for information security

That the organizations understand the need for information security is another success factor that was identified:

"...that the company becomes aware of a need to protect its own, its customers and other stakeholders information."

"...understanding that the management system for information security must cover the whole organization"

"management's understanding..."

Although this factor may seem trivial, it is mentioned many times by the respondents. They sometimes perceive a lack of appreciation of the importance of information security from parts of the organization.

5) Motivated employees
Some of the answers focused on the need to motivate employees:

"To motivate the employees to develop processes and procedures within their own areas of responsibility. ..."

"...motivated project management /-participants. ..."

The answers focus on the motivation of individuals participating in the ISMS project, such as project participants, project managers, and those responsible for different areas in the organization. After the development of the ISMS, it will also have to be implemented, and at that stage the importance of this success factor grow – at that time, *all* employees in the whole organization will have to be motivated to adhere to the rules. Further, they should regularly use the technical solutions that the projects have developed and the management decided on – they need motivation.

6) Access to external competence
The final success factor identified by the questionnaires was the importance of being able to call for external competence when needed:

"...good reference persons (preferably certification authorities from the beginning)."

" ... access to external specialist competence."

This factor is concerned with both experts and advisors in IT- and information security, but also about opening the dialog between the

organization and the certification authority at an early stage. This contact –
organization vs. certification authority – must be seen as very important – at
least if the organization is planning to seek certification of its ISMS after the
implementation.

Summary

The certification auditors in the Swedish pilot certification group viewed
these six factors as critical for the successful implementation and
certification of ISMS:

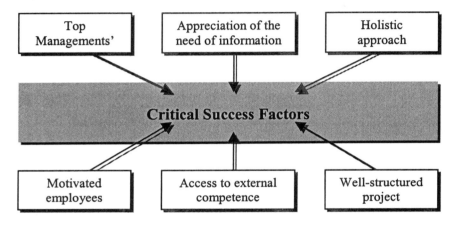

Figure 1: Critical Success Factors for the implementation and certification of information
security management systems, from the certification auditors' perspective.

4.   INFORMATION SECURITY CONSULTANTS' PERSPECTIVE ON IMPLEMENTATION AND CERTIFICATION OF ISMS

Also for this group, the question was stated as follows (translation from
Swedish to English):

```
In your opinion, which are the critical success
factors for a successful implementation of an
information security management system, ISMS?
```

Also here, the answers were analyzed using a grounded theory method
supported by a computerized data analysis tool (ATLAS/ti).

In total, there were 37 quotations from the consultants on this question. They were first analyzed and coded into 23 different categories, using no predetermined codes. This means that the essence of each quote can be represented by its code on this level. Afterwards, these 23 categories were further analyzed using the qualitative data analysis tool and we found that they fell into 6 more abstract categories.

Even though all the answers were in Swedish, we decided to code each quotation in English, so that it would be easier to present in this paper. However, the answers were not translated, but they are available in the Swedish report for those interested (draft, forthcoming).

It should be noted that there is no logic in the data analysis tool to help deciding on the categories of the data. The tool is only used to organize the analysis, and to keep track of and visualize the analysis result.

Here are all the codes used at the *first* level of analysis:

- ability to put policy into practice
- accurate analysis of preceding security situation
- active employee participation
- active project members
- appropriate project organization
- backing from top management
- balanced policy grounded in reality
- clear aim from top management
- customer organization participation
- documented business processes
- feasible implementation method
- identifiable business benefits
- implementation know-how for project leader
- insight and knowledge about security
- integration with existing management systems
- monetary resources
- project ability to influence IT development
- realistic cost estimation
- realistic time plans
- regular communication with stakeholders
- top management awareness
- top management involvement
- understanding the need for security

These codes were further analyzed and categorized into six more abstract categories. These six categories were:

- ❑ Project management capability
- ❑ Commanding capability
- ❑ Financial capability
- ❑ Analytic capability
- ❑ Communicative capability
- ❑ Executive capability

These capabilities form the foundation for a theoretical framework. Here is a short description of each of these capabilities.

Project management capability. A successful implementation project will need to have efficient project management capability. This means that for example active project members, an appropriate project organization and realistic time plans are needed.

Commanding capability. The commanding capability stems from the top management sponsorship of the project. It is this capability that gives the project the authority to decide on issues regarding information security. Without any real decision-making power, it is very hard, if not impossible to do reach the project goals. This capability is given by for example top management awareness and involvement in information security, identifiable business benefits and an understanding for the need of security, and a clear aim and backing from top management.

Financial capability. All information security projects need budgeted resources. A project with this capability is able to estimate costs realistically. It also has access to the resources needed to carry out the project.

Analytic capability. Projects with analytic capability can accurately analyse the preceding security situation, and therefore develop a well balanced ISMS which is also integrated with existing management systems (e.g. quality and environment management systems – iso900X and iso1400X). In short, this capability is needed to create a balanced policy grounded in reality.

Communicative capability. Many information security efforts stop at the security managers' desk. To avoid this, a communicative capability is needed. This capability is needed to enable regular communication with stakeholders and for active employee participation in the project.

Executive capability. Thinking about security and writing policies is one thing – implementing the ideas, rules, controls, and procedures is another. The executive capability means that the project can do things – that it can make things happen. One of the things that will need to be done is to put the policy into practice and this in turn often requires for example the ability to influence people in the IT department, in IT development and in other parts of the organization. A feasible implementation method and implementation know-how for the project leader are examples of parts that form this capability.

Summary
The information security consultants of the Swedish pilot certification group viewed these six capabilities as critical for the successful implementation and certification of ISMS:

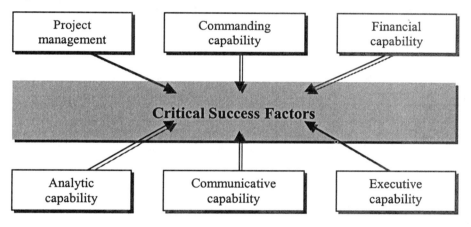

Figure2: Critical Success Factors for the implementation and certification of information security management systems, from the information security consultants' perspective.

To demonstrate visually how this theoretical framework was developed, and how it is related with the data from the questionnaires, please refer to the network diagram in appendix 1.

5.   CONCLUSIONS

Using an action research strategy and a grounded theory research method, this study has identified critical success factors for the implementation and certification of information security management systems. Even though we cannot statistically generalize these findings to a broader population, we believe that these results can be useful and valid. Especially for researchers and practitioners working with 7799 and similar management standards.

6.   REFERENCES

BSI (1999): BS 7799-1:1999, Information security management. Code of practice for information security management (This standard is now withdrawn and superseded by "BS ISO/IEC 17799:2000, BS 7799-1:2000, Information technology. Code of practice for information security management"), 1999, British Standards Institution: London.

Denscombe M (1998): The Good Research Guide. Open University Press: Buckingham.

Eloff M and S. Von Solms (1998): Measuring the information security level in an organisation, in Proceedings of the sixth working conference of IFIP WG 11.1 and 11.2, Budapest, 1998.

Eloff, M. and S. Von Solms (2000a): Information Security: Process Evaluation and Product Evaluation. In Qing, S., and J. Eloff, 2000: Information Security for Global Information Infrastructures (Proceedings of the IFIP TC11 16th annual working conference on information security during the World Computer Congress, Beijing, August 21-25 2000). Amsterdam: Kluwer Academic Publishers

Eloff, M. and S. Von Solms (2000b): Information Security Management: An Approach to Combine Process Certification And Product Evaluation. Journal of Computers and Security, Vol. 19, Issue 8, Pages 698-709 Elsevier Science Ltd.

Glaser, B. and A. Strauss (1967): The Discovery of Grounded Theory. Chicago: Aldine.

ISO (2000): ISO/IEC 17799:2000, Information technology -- Code of practice for information security management, 2000, International Organization for Standardization (ISO), Geneva, Switzerland.

Labuschagne (draft, forthcoming): Web Assurance: Information security management for e-commerce. Draft available at http://csweb.rau.ac.za/deth/research/index.htm, Accessed 2001-03-28.

Siponen (2001): On the scientific background of information security management standards: a critique and an agenda for further development. The Second Annual Systems Security Engineering Conference (SSE), 28 February - 2 March, Orlando, Florida, USA.

SIS (1999): SS 62 77 99: Ledningssystem för informationssäkerhet - Del 1: Riktlinjer för ledning av informationssäkerhet, 1999, Swedish Standards Institute (SIS), Stockholm, Sweden. (Swedish translation of BSI, 1999)

R von Solms (1999): Information security management: why standards are important. Information Management and Computer Security, Vol 7 Issue 1 Date 1999.

S von Solms (2000): Information Security - The Third Wave?, Computers & Security, Volume 19, Issue 7, 1 November 2000, Pages 615-620

Strauss, A. and J. Corbin (1994): Grounded theory methodology – An Overview. In Denzin and Lincoln, Handbook of Qualitative Research, Sage, Pages 273-285).

Susman G., and R. Evered (1978): An assessment of the scientific merits of action research. Administrative Science Quarterly, 23(4): 582-603.

Appendix 1: Information security consultants' view

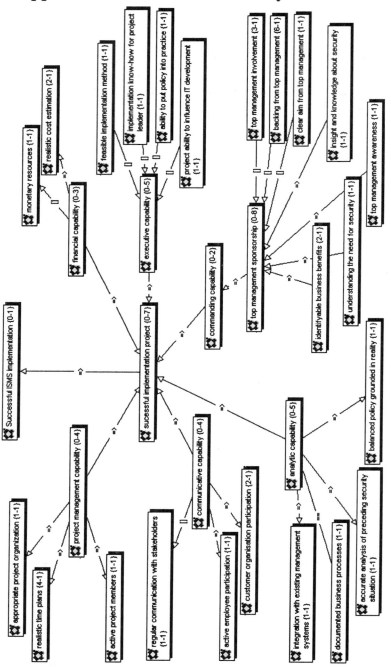

INDEX OF CONTRIBUTORS